LEAVING CERTIF

Music Revision

Andrew Purcell

GILL EDUCATION

Gill Education
Hume Avenue
Park West
Dublin 12
www.gilleducation.ie
Gill Education is an imprint of M.H. Gill & Co.

© Andrew Purcell 2011

978 07171 4687 1

Design by Liz White Designs.
Artwork by Oxford Designers & Illustrators.
Music artwork by Halstan Music Setting.
Print origination by Carrigboy Typesetting Services.

The paper used in this book is made from the wood pulp of managed forests. For every
tree felled, at least one tree is planted, thereby renewing natural resources.

CONTENTS

Note: Material that is to be studied only by those taking Higher level is indicated in the text.

Introduction

How the Exam is marked

There are **400 marks** (100%) available for the entire Leaving Certificate Music examination.

Core Practical

This accounts for **100 marks** (25% of the total). It is usually examined just before or after Easter holidays during school time.

Listening Paper

Marks available: **100 marks** (25% of the total). These are distributed as follows:

- Set Works
  - Question 1 (long question): 25 marks (6.25%) of the total exam.
  - Questions 2, 3 and 4: 10 marks each, which amounts to 30 marks (7.5% of the complete exam).
- Question 5: Irish Traditional Music
  - 25 marks (6.25% of the total exam).
  - At Higher level, 15 marks are available for the Listening component and 10 marks are available for the essay-style question.
- Question 6: Aural Skills
  - 20 marks (5% of the total exam).

Composition Paper

Marks available: **100 marks** (25% of the total). These are distributed as follows:

- Melody question (Question 1 *or* 2 *or* 3): 40 marks (10% of the total exam).
- Harmony question (Question 4 *or* 5 *or* 6): 60 marks (15% of the total exam).

Elective (Higher level only): Practical, Listening or Composition

Marks available: **100 marks** (25% of the total exam).

Choose *one* Elective from:
- Practical: This is done with the Core Practical and includes Music Technology or Conducting electives if chosen.
- Composition: This is portfolio work.
- Listening Elective: This is a 45-minute written paper on the day of the core exams in June. It comes after the Listening and Composition core papers.

Ordinary level candidates do **not** have to take an elective. Their highest mark in core Listening, Composition **or** Practical will be doubled to make up the extra 25% for their overall grade.

It is really important to understand the **marking scheme** for the exam. The Higher and Ordinary level Listening and Composition papers are very **similar** in marking set-up and correction and have changed very little in terms of layout and content for many years. Please be aware that the exam layout and **content is liable to change at any time**, once it complies with the Leaving Certificate Music **syllabus**.

IN THE EXAM HALL

- Fill in your examination number and follow all instructions on the exam paper.

- In the Listening examination, the first excerpt on the CD will be to **make sure that you are able to hear** the music perfectly in whatever room or hall you are sitting your exam. If you have a problem hearing the music on the CD, don't be afraid to let the supervisor know immediately, so that it can be fixed promptly.

- Read through all the Listening paper questions.

- Observe the given melody lines, keys, etc. in the Composing questions.

- Highlight the **key words** in each question.

- Note the **command word** – circle, describe, state, explain, find, suggest, list, etc. Example: 'state and describe' means state and then describe fully, so write a few sentences.

- **Allocate your time carefully.** There is no need to rush, as you have 1 hour and 30 minutes for these exams.

- Don't leave early! Go back and make sure you have answered every question fully. There is time after the CD is completed to finish and go back over all your answers.

- All musical notations that you have written should be correct and as **neat** as possible.

- Use a sharp B pencil when composing.

- Answer the written questions in blue or black pen.

- Attempt the correct number of questions in the Composition paper. You can answer more than one Melody (Questions 1, 2 or 3) and one Harmony question (Questions 4, 5 or 6) but it is better to make sure you attempt **one fully** than try to rush through two or three incomplete answers!

- Study the given melody and harmony bars in detail. For example: sing the given bars *in your head* a number of times before deciding on any rhythm for your answering phrase, bass line, etc.

USEFUL WEBSITES

- The State Examination Commission's website is *www.examinations.ie.* Here you will find invaluable resources, such as: *General Guidelines for Music* (information notes); previous examination papers and musical excerpts; marking schemes; Chief Examiner's reports; unprepared tests, etc.

- The Leaving Certificate Music syllabus and Guidelines for Teachers are available from the Department of Education and Skills website (*www.education.ie*).

- The PPMTA (Post Primary Music Teachers' Association) runs local workshops and an annual conference for music teachers. Student revision courses are also run each spring. Lots of information is available on *www.ppmta.ie.*

1 How to Handle the Set Works on the Listening Paper

aims

- To learn how to answer the Listening Paper questions properly and with confidence.

Students and teachers: remember that it is the Leaving Certificate Music **syllabus** (not the past examination papers) that states all the goals and objectives that should be reached after **five years** of music tuition in the classroom. It's worth looking at what the syllabus says about the Set Works examined in the Listening Paper.

2.3.2 Prescribed works

Ordinary level and Higher level students **must** study **all four works** from the appropriate list …

Prescribed works should be studied **in detail**. In the case of each work, students must:

- understand, identify and describe the range of musical features used
- study its musical style and place it in its historical context
- be able to analyse and describe patterns of repetition and change within the music.

In studying each prescribed work, **Higher level students** must also demonstrate an ability to:

- make comparative judgements about music
- evaluate interpretation and performance in the light of experience already attained.

Leaving Certificate Music syllabus (1996)

The Department of Education's *Music – Leaving Certificate Guidelines for Teachers* also makes the following points (under 4.3 Prescribed works):

The following list of features will further help students (and teachers) to identify appropriate content:

- Rudiments – e.g. rhythm, metre, pitch, melody, dynamics, speeds, harmony, cadences, texture, terms, signs and abbreviations.
- Structures/form – e.g. binary, ternary, sonata, minuet and trio, variation, rondo.
- Composing techniques – e.g. ostinato, sequence, imitation, antiphony.
- Instrumental techniques – e.g. pizzicato, piano clusters, harmonic.
- Voices and instruments.
- Ensembles.
- Musical genres.
- Styles and periods.

Students must also be able to recognise all note and rest values and all terminology, musical signs and symbols used in all scores of their four prescribed works.

Key features to be familiar with in all Set Works

You must have a clear understanding of:

- form
- instrumentation
- style/genre
- texture
- historical periods and characteristics of each musical period
- key signatures and tonality of sections and themes and musical excerpts
- tempo
- cadence points (visual and aural recognition of them)
- rhythmic features
- melodic features
- time signature
- dynamics (and contrasts between sections)
- instrumental and compositional devices or techniques.

All the key musical characteristics and the terminology associated with them are covered in detail in **Chapter 3** of this book. It is very important to understand each feature and its relevant terms (musical terminology, signs and symbols), and to be able to recognise these features **aurally**.

Time management

- Do you spend too long studying and analysing each Set Work in class and at home?
- Remember: the four Set Works questions on the Listening Paper combined amount to just 55 marks. That is just 13.75% of the total marks for the course.
- To put this percentage in context: your four Set Works questions are worth less than the single Harmony question (60 marks)!
- With this in mind, have you got an appropriate study time plan in place?

Sample study sessions for Tchaikovsky's *Romeo and Juliet* *Fantasy Overture*

> **key point**
>
> Be aware of your own level of knowledge, learning capabilities and understanding of musical features and create your own study plan based on that.

Study Session 1

Time: 35 minutes

Aim: To understand the musical concepts through aural skill work.

- Listen to the overture as if you were completing an Aural Skills Question 6.
- Simply turn on your CD and write down everything that you hear!
- Identify instruments, texture, tempo, dynamics, rhythmic and melodic features.
- Listen to the overture twice in one session.

Study Session 2

Time: 20 minutes

Aim: To understand the structure of sonata form as used in the overture.

- Begin to identify musically the many themes and developments of compositional ideas (melodic/rhythmic).
- Try to put together a CD of short excerpts of all the main themes for this study session.
- Take notes as you listen to each theme and use these notes to analyse musical features.

Study Session 3

Time: 1 hour, split over two study sessions

Aim: To improve score reading skills.

- Listen to your CD while following your score.
- Write or highlight any important points in your score.
- Complete homework assignments from your teacher or from Leaving Certificate Music workbooks.
- Remember: a blank score is an unused score!

Study Session 4

Time: Variable

Aim: To explore existing analyses of the overture.

- Read 'official' analysis of the overture.
- Source Curriculum Support Team notes online.
- Read analyses from a variety of textbooks.
- Always analyse the music with reference to a recording!

Study Session 5

Time: Variable

Aim: To analyse past exam questions on the overture.

- Source as many previous exam papers as you can find.
- Analyse the types of questions asked.
- Find the answers and marking schemes and use them to assess your own answers.

Study Session 6

Time: 25 minutes: 10 minutes for test and 15 minutes for correction

Aim: Self-assessment using a past exam paper.

- Your teacher can help you to source a question and a CD excerpt that you haven't already worked on.
- Complete the exam question in the time allowed.
- You can correct your own work (using the relevant marking scheme) or ask your teacher or a classmate to correct it for you.
- This will give you an insight into how well prepared for the exam you are.

Active listening and active learning

When studying your four Set Works, try to treat them as an unknown Aural Skills question (Question 6 in the Listening Paper). Try to learn, study and revise all of the important musical characteristics of each Set Work by **active featured listening**.

Below are some ideas for **active learning**. Some of these ideas work best if you can study in small groups of 'critical friends' (classmates and friends who are focused on the same outcome as you).

- Don't get too worried about the huge amount of notes that your teacher has given you or the indepth analysis in textbooks. That's not to say that you should ignore the notes! Just try to remember that you are sitting a listening examination.

- Listen to the prescribed music in a feature-based way. Every time you listen to the music, focus on **one** particular musical feature. For example: in one particular study session, listen only to the **texture**. In another study session, listen only to the **accompaniment**. In the next study session, listen only to the way that the **melodic line** moves. It is hard to keep this focus in each study session, but it really is a worthwhile exercise.

- Get some **musical variety**! Download different versions of your Set Works. There are dozens of versions of the Set Works available online. Don't listen to your Set Works only in class. You **must** make an effort to listen to them in your own time. By listening to many different versions of your Set Works, you will not be put out by the excerpts that are played in the actual Listening examination.

- Know how your music sounds – in your head! Spend time learning to sing/hum the main melodies of your Set Works. Really get to know them; **don't always rely on the CD** to do the work for you.

- If you are not good at following the scores of your Set Works and you keep getting lost, don't worry. **Simplify it by magnifying it!** Try photocopying some important themes of the score on big A3 sheets. Then stick them up on the wall of your study area, so that you can see them clearly as you listen to your prescribed music.

- Have a score-reading competition with your classmates based on **musical bars** rather than musical chairs! One student stops and starts the CD at ten different points, while the other students write down the bar numbers where the music stopped.

- Study and revision can be **fun**. Use quizzes, crosswords and word searches as revision work. Making these is also a good learning experience. For hints and tips, visit websites such as *www.discoveryeducation.com/free-puzzlemaker*.

- It is vital for you to understand **what kind of learner** you are. Visit websites such as *www.vark-learn.com* to help you identify this and to build study plans that suit you. Revision aids such as spidergrams, mnemonics, mind maps, brainstorming and group study sessions can be really helpful.

Other **learning methodologies and aids** that you might use when studying your Set Works are listed below.

1. Co-operative Learning

- Question and answer sessions amongst classmates and friends.
- Sharing study plans or revision aids (e.g. spidergrams) with other students in your class.
- Open discussion sessions between students and teachers regarding the Set Works.

2. Research

You could choose project work for your Listening Elective option. Examples of suitable project areas include: Romantic overtures, Baroque cantatas, French programme music, classical piano concerti, contemporary Irish instrumental music, etc. Research work for a project will inform your listening experience for the Set Works.

3. I.C.T.

- Embrace music technology! Notating themes from your Set Works into software packages such as Sibelius or Finale is worthwhile. This is a particularly good idea if you are taking Music Technology as a Performing option.
- The internet is a fantastic resource for learning about Set Works, composers, instruments and historical contexts.

4. Assessment and evaluation

Correcting music homework that your friends or classmates have done is excellent for revision. You learn by identifying mistakes!

5. Live performance

You will develop musical awareness by attending live performances. Can you or any of your class perform some or all of the more accessible sections of your prescribed works? This can be great fun, as well as a fantastic learning experience!

Multi-tasking

On the day of the exam, you will be expected to do some **focused multi-tasking!** If you wish to gain high marks on this paper, you will have to do **four tasks** for each part of each question or excerpt.

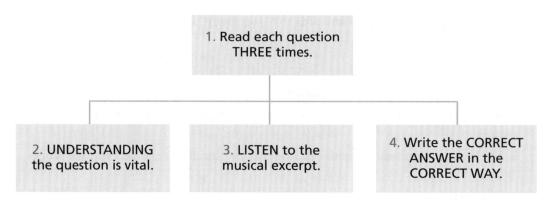

1. Read each question THREE times.

2. UNDERSTANDING the question is vital.

3. LISTEN to the musical excerpt.

4. Write the CORRECT ANSWER in the CORRECT WAY.

1. Carefully read the question three times.
2. Think about what exactly the question asks of you. Highlight or underline important words in the text. If musical notation is given, identify the important bars that relate to your question.
3. Listen intently and in a highly concentrated manner to the extract played. In your mind, process the information using correct musical terminology.
4. Write the correct answer in a suitable way: tick a box, fill in a blank space, describe, identify, state, etc.

exam focus

Don't spend too long on any one part of a question. The answer to another part of the question may be played in the musical excerpt while your focus is still on the previous question! If you know your Set Works well enough, you will be able to come back to finish a question at the end of the aural excerpts in the examination.

Listening exam tactics

- There should be no need for you to **interpret** the questions posed on the Listening Paper. The questions are usually straightforward, if you understand what you are being asked and how you should answer. Answer questions in a clear and concise fashion using correct musical terminology.

- There are **short questions** in this section, such as: tick the box, underline the correct word, etc. Also in this category are **closed questions**, which begin with words such as 'identify' or 'state'. These questions need a short answer only, whether it is one word or a brief description of a musical term, etc.

- There is **no need** (and little space) **for you to waffle on**, especially if you end up writing some incorrect information. Don't make the mistake of writing the names of five instruments if the question has asked you to identify only three! This is similar to ticking two boxes when asked to tick one only. The cancellation of marks may apply in some cases.

- If you don't know a 'tick the box' answer, you should at least have a guess. **Never leave any part of an answer paper blank.**

- It's best not to change your mind on a 'tick the box' question. It is statistically proven that the first answer that pops into your head is, more often than not, the correct one!

- If you make a mess of a 'tick the box' question and start scribbling out your original tick, be very clear about which choice you finally arrive at. Really spell it out for the corrector.

- Long questions such as 'describe', 'comment on' and 'discuss' obviously need longer answers. Aim to answer with **three pieces of correct information**, using **correct musical terminology** backed up with a **description of what is happening in the CD excerpt** at that point. Avoid generic answers here.

Sample exam questions and answers explained

HIGHER LEVEL QUESTION 3 (IV), 2008   HL

Mozart: Piano Concerto in A Major K488

(iv) Comment on the texture of the music from bar 9.
Sample answer 1: This excerpt is mainly **homophonic**. The first violins play the main melody accompanied by pedal notes in the lower strings and long notes in the woodwind and horns. Near the end of the excerpt there is a new theme – a repeating antiphonal section between the strings and woodwind.

Sample answer 2: Homophonic – melody with accompaniment.

Comments:

- The first sample answer is much better than the second. While sample answer 2 is factually correct, it may not score full marks.

HIGHER LEVEL QUESTION 1, EXCERPT 1, PART (II), 2008

Berlioz: Symphonie Fantastique

(ii) Identify two features of the melody in this excerpt.

Comments:

- Your answer should involve identification of two melodic features, using musicals terms and giving a description. For example: ascending or descending scales or scalic movement; chromatic or triadic movement; repeated or repeating notes; specific interval jumps, etc.
- Two or three pieces of correct information would suffice.
- Don't write about rhythmic or textural features, or about instruments playing the accompaniment.
- Deal only with the question asked. Be focused and always answer with the most obvious (which is usually the most simple) response.

HIGHER LEVEL QUESTION 2 (V), 2008

The Beatles: Sgt. Pepper's Lonely Hearts Club Band

(v) Contrast the style of 'When I'm Sixty-Four' with the other two songs by The Beatles on your course. Refer to all three songs in your answer.

Sample answer 1: 'When I'm Sixty-Four' is a fusion of pop/jazz, clearly defined by the use of jazzy clarinets bending notes and the use of brushes instead of drumsticks. 'Sgt. Pepper's Lonely Hearts Club Band' is also a pop song but is fused with rock and classical elements (rock beat and vocals and use of polyphonic French horns), while 'She's Leaving Home' is a pop song fused with classical style elements (the string nonet instrumentation).

Sample answer 2: 'When I'm Sixty-Four' is a fusion of pop/jazz, the others aren't!

Comments:

- 'Compare and contrast' questions require a careful approach. You must always refer to each part of the excerpt when answering *each* element of the question.
- Sample answer 1 is thorough and it answers each part of the question. Sample answer 2 is unlikely to gain many marks.

Many successful students divide their answer into easily identifiable sections when answering 'compare and contrast' questions. Some even draw tables or grids with appropriate columns and rows to make sure that all parts of the question are responded to in full.

Common errors in Listening examination answers

- **Ticking too few or too many boxes** or circling/underlining too many notes or words. Doing this means that you may get a mark deducted, so read your question very carefully!
- **Blank spaces in long questions** don't look well. Make sure you fill up the space allowed with three pieces of correct information and a simple description of what you hear on the CD.
- **Not attempting melodic/rhythmic dictation.** Always attempt these questions and bear in mind that sometimes there is something similar already printed in the exam paper, e.g. a musical sequence.
- **Notating too many or too few notes** in a dictation question. You may be told that there are only five notes to be notated. If this is so, there is no point in notating ten notes!
- No difference in answering style for **closed** and **open** questions.
- Lack of understanding of musical **terminology** used in the question.
- Incomplete answers to **compare and contrast** questions.

2 Understanding Musical Characteristics

aims

- To gain knowledge of musical analysis and the musical terminology used to answer questions in the Set Works, Aural Skills and Irish Music sections and also in Performance and Composition.

Historical periods

Orchestra seating chart: Baroque period

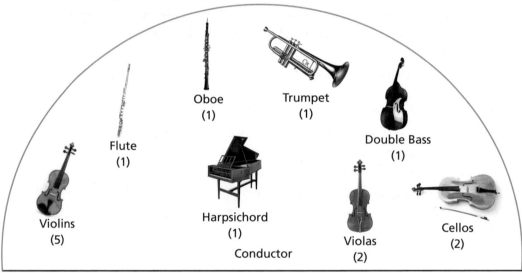

Oboe
(1)

Trumpet
(1)

Double Bass
(1)

Flute
(1)

Harpsichord
(1)

Violins
(5)

Conductor

Violas
(2)

Cellos
(2)

Orchestra seating chart: Classical period

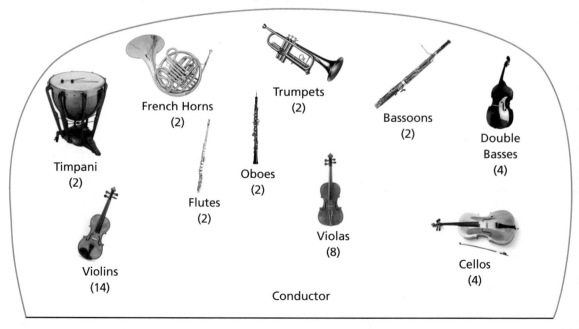

French Horns
(2)

Trumpets
(2)

Bassoons
(2)

Double
Basses
(4)

Timpani
(2)

Oboes
(2)

Flutes
(2)

Violas
(8)

Cellos
(4)

Violins
(14)

Conductor

Orchestra seating chart: Romantic period

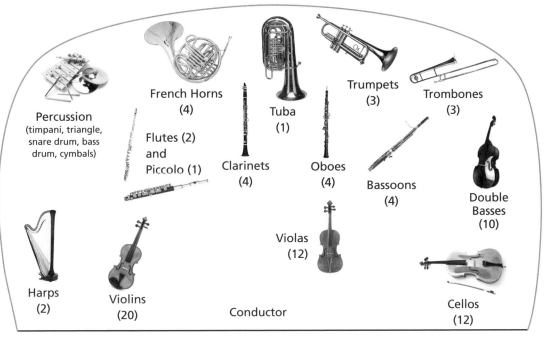

Orchestra seating chart: Modern period

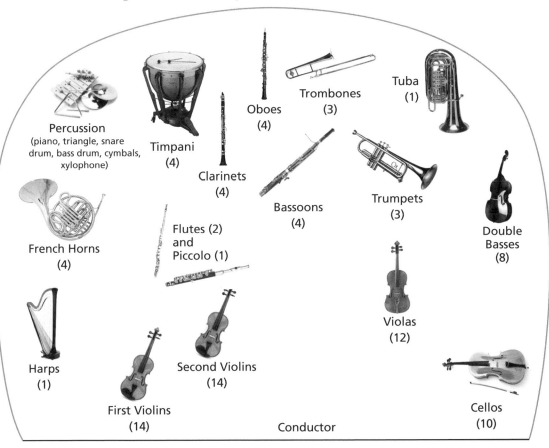

Medieval – c. 800–1400

- use of modes
- monophonic textures – Gregorian chant
- contrasting timbres of medieval instruments
- later more elaborate polyphonic textures – motets
- introduction of harmony.

Renaissance – c. 1450–1600

- rich variety of pieces, both sacred and secular
- mainly vocal forms but also instrumental dances
- more complex textures – four-part vocal counterpoint, lots of imitation
- blending of timbres
- use of modes, but major and minor are more prominent.

Baroque – c. 1600–1750

- major/minor key system instigated
- mainly complex polyphonic forms – counterpoint, canon, fugue
- choral music and instrumental dance forms are most important
- figured bass (basso continuo) used in most music
- only one mood per section or piece
- terraced dynamic levels used
- much use of ornamentation in long melodic phrases
- lively, fast rhythms.

Classical – c. 1750–1820

- increase in use of piano and decreased use of harpsichord
- instrumental music forms (symphony, concerto, sonata, string quartet) develop into structured designs
- clear texture (usually homophonic) with melody (short, balanced phrases) and melodic development important
- set number of instrumentalists in organised orchestra.

Romantic – c. 1820–1900

- expansion of the orchestra, development of instruments
- greater technical virtuosity by instrumentalists
- adventurous harmonies with lyrical melodies
- larger contrast in textures, dynamics and timbre

- programme music – more personal compositional styles
- huge variety of pieces and genres – from chamber music and song cycles to huge symphonic works and operas.

Impressionist – c. 1880–1920

- modal scales (pentatonic, whole tone scales) and unusual harmonies
- fluid, shifting melodies – no clear-cut form or phrase
- colourful orchestral timbres.

Modern – c.1900–present

- huge variety in styles
- atonal music – serial, electronic, aleatoric music
- tonal music – neo-classicism, minimalism
- many iconoclastic composers with their own individual styles
- huge mixture of instrumental/vocal ensembles
- fusion with popular, folk, jazz and rock music styles
- film music and musicals very prominent
- personalities very important (performers, conductors, composers and orchestras).

Style/Genre

Style describes the characteristic way composers of different eras compose a piece of music: the way the many musical elements of melody, rhythm, harmony, timbre, texture, form, tempo, etc. are put together to form a piece of music, whether a baroque chorale or a modern film score.

What words can you use to describe the 'style' or 'genre' of a given extract?

- classical
- vocal
- operatic
- symphonic
- instrumental
- popular
- rock
- folk

- traditional
- blues
- electronic music
- ethnic
- non-Western
- jazz/jazzy
- programme music
- film music

- absolute music
- fusion
- musical
- Oriental
- secular
- sacred.

key point

Listen to as many musical styles as possible. Try to label each piece of music you hear with a **stylistic description**.

Dynamics

Dynamics means the loudness or quietness of a sound. You must interpret each dynamic marking depending on:

- comparison with other dynamics in the music
- the dynamic range for that instrument or ensemble
- the ability of the performer(s).

Traditionally, dynamic markings are based on Italian words.

Typical Dynamic Markings

ppp pp p   *mp*   *mf*   *f   ff   fff*

p = piano, soft   *m* = mezzo, moderately   *f* = forte, loud

If the composer wants the change from one dynamic level to another to be gradual, different markings are added. A *crescendo* (cresc.) means 'gradually get louder'; a *decrescendo* or *diminuendo* (dim.) means 'gradually get softer'. These markings also mean *crescendo* and *diminuendo*:

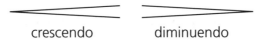

            crescendo   diminuendo

key point

As a general rule, each dynamic level that is louder or softer than the previous level should be **twice** as loud or soft: *ff* should be approximately twice as loud as *f*.

HINTS

- In *melody composition* you must insert appropriate dynamic markings for the entire 16-bar melody (or 8-bar at Ordinary level), not just for your own written 12 bars.
- In much music, the dynamics decrease at the cadence point (especially at a suspension/resolution) but a strong, final perfect cadence may be loud to very loud.
- When inputting dynamics, it is sometimes useful to follow the shape of the melodic line, especially at the climax: a crescendo is easier to play with an ascending motion than a descending scale, for example.
- There is no need to insert dynamics in every bar – one, two or three markings per phrase is more than enough.

A *crescendo* or *diminuendo* hairpin must be preceded by an appropriate dynamic marking. The *crescendo* or *diminuendo* hairpin must then go to another appropriate dynamic level.

Dynamics – instrument ranges

When inserting dynamics for your melody, be careful of using dynamic levels that are nearly impossible to play on certain instruments. For example: an *fff* marking for a flute playing its lowest notes or a *pp* marking for a very high trumpet opening is inappropriate as it is nearly impossible to play well. So:

- learn the ranges of instruments/voices (*tessitura*)
- use comfortable dynamic markings (*pp* to *ff*) in your melody composition.

Articulation

Articulation is how one sings or plays the notes of a piece. Exactly how each articulation should be played depends on the instrument playing it, as well as on the style and period of the music.

Accents are markings that are used to indicate especially strong-sounding notes with a definite attack. Some accents may even be played by making the note longer or more separate from the other notes, rather than just louder. The exact performance of each type of accent depends on the instrument and the style and period of the music, but the *sforzando (sfz)* and *fortepiano (fp)*-type accents are usually louder and longer, and more likely to be used in a long note that starts loudly and then suddenly gets much softer.

- *Staccato* – short, detached notes. Dot under or over the note only.
- *Marcato* – stressed, accented notes.
- *Legato* – the opposite of staccato. Smooth, connected series of notes (varies in string or wind playing).
- *Slur* – only the first note of a set of slurred notes has a definite articulation. All other notes under the slur are played *legato*.
- *No articulation marking* – Much music has little or no articulation marking.

Notes can be played separated or, more commonly, it is up to the performer to interpret the music in a correct stylistic manner.

Phrase marks and/or articulation markings are needed for the Melody Composition question. If using articulation marks, make sure you understand how your markings will affect the performance of the piece by the instrument that you chose.

Tempo

The **tempo** of a piece of music is the speed at which it is played. There are two ways to specify a tempo:

- **Metronome markings** are absolute and specific.
- **Verbal descriptions** are more relative and subjective.

Metronome markings are given in beats per minute. Tempo instructions are usually given in Italian.

Some common tempo markings:

- **grave** – very slow and solemn
- **largo** – slow and broad
- **larghetto** – not quite as slow as largo
- **adagio** – slow
- **lento** – slow
- **andante** – literally 'walking', a medium slow tempo
- **moderato** – moderate, or medium
- **allegretto** – not as fast as allegro
- **allegro** – fast
- **vivo** or **vivace** – lively and brisk
- **presto** – very fast
- **prestissimo** – very, very fast.

More useful Italian terms:

- **poco** – a little
- **molto** – a lot
- **più** – more
- **meno** – less
- **mosso** – literally 'moved'; movement
- **rallentando** (**rall.**) or **ritardando** (**rit.**) – slow down
- **accelerando** (**accel.**) – speed up.

Texture

When you describe the texture of a piece of music, you are describing how much is going on in the music at any given moment. For example, the texture of a piece of music may have many or just one or two layers. It might be made up of rhythm alone, or of a melody line with chordal accompaniment, or many interweaving melodies.

Terms that describe texture:

- dense/rich
- thin/sparse
- monophonic or monophony
- homophonic or homophony
- polyphonic or polyphony
- counterpoint
- contrapuntal
- countermelody
- descant
- canon or canonic
- fugue or fugal
- stretto
- heterophony
- antiphonal.

Monophonic music has only one melodic line, with no harmony or counterpoint. There may be rhythmic accompaniment, but only one line that has specific pitches; plainchant is one example.

Homophonic music has one clearly melodic line; it is the most important line musically. All other parts provide accompaniment of one type or another. There may be some melodic interest in the accompaniment parts but it is clear that they are not independent melodic parts, either because they have the same rhythm as the melody (i.e. are not independent) or because their main purpose is to fill in the chords or harmony (i.e. they are not really melodies).

Polyphonic music can also be called counterpoint, or contrapuntal music. If more than one independent melody is occurring at the same time, the music is polyphonic.

Examples of polyphonic music:

- Rounds, canons, and fugues: even if there is only one melody, if different people are singing or playing it at different times, the parts sound independent.
- Much baroque music is contrapuntal (e.g. parts of the Aria Duet in J. S. Bach's Cantata BWV 78).
- Most music for large instrumental groups such as bands or orchestras is contrapuntal at least some of the time.
- Music that is mostly homophonic can become temporarily polyphonic if an independent countermelody is added.

Musical textures

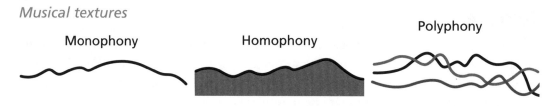

Monophony   Homophony   Polyphony

Cadences

A cadence is a place in a piece of music that feels like a **stopping or resting point**. It is made up of two chords (sometimes with an approach chord). There are four types of cadence, depending on what chord progressions are used.

Cadences end phrases or sections of music and so the form/structure of a piece is closely linked to cadential points. Most tonal pieces use regularly spaced cadences (and phrasing) in a 4–8–16–32-bar pattern.

When trying to identify cadences in a listening extract, ask yourself:
1. Does it sound *finished* or *unfinished*?
2. Does it end in a major or minor chord?
3. Is it a strong ending or a weak ending?
4. Does the music feel unresolved (i.e. as though it needs to carry on)?

Changes in the rhythm of a piece, a pause in the rhythm, a lengthening of the note values or a slowing of the harmonic rhythm are often found at cadence points.

Name	Major Key	Minor Key
Perfect Cadence Strong final sound	V—I Use in root position at end of piece	V—i Chord V always has accidental in minor key
Plagal Cadence Sounds like *A-men* at the end of a hymn	IV—I	iv—I Minor to minor
Imperfect Cadence Ends on dominant chord	I or ii or IV—V	I or iv—V
Interrupted Cadence Tonality change – unexpected sound	V—vi Major to minor chord in a major key	V—VI Major to major chord in a minor key

Intervals

An interval is the distance between two pitches. The name of an interval depends both on how the notes are written and the actual distance between the notes as measured in semitones.

The first step in naming the interval is to find the distance between the notes *as they are written on the stave*. For example, the interval between G and C is a fourth; the interval between F and E is a seventh.

Perfect intervals

Unison, octaves, fourths and fifths can be perfect intervals:

> **key point**
>
> **Compound intervals are larger than an octave.**

Perfect intervals

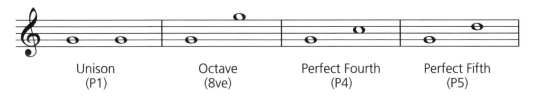

| Unison (P1) | Octave (8ve) | Perfect Fourth (P4) | Perfect Fifth (P5) |

Major and minor intervals

Seconds, thirds, sixths, and sevenths can be major intervals or minor intervals. The minor interval is always a semitone smaller than the major interval.

- 1 semitone = minor second (m2)
- 2 semitones = major second (M2)
- 3 semitones = minor third (m3)
- 4 semitones = major third (M3)
- 8 semitones= minor sixth (m6)
- 9 semitones = major sixth (M6)
- 10 semitones = minor seventh (m7)
- 11 semitones = major seventh (M7)
- 12 semitones = perfect octave (P8)

Major and minor intervals

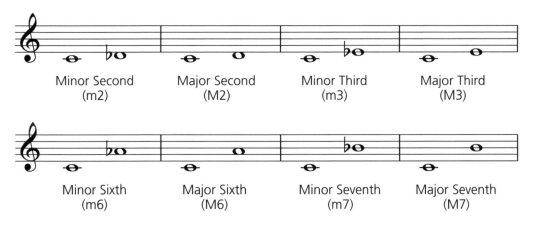

| Minor Second (m2) | Major Second (M2) | Minor Third (m3) | Major Third (M3) |

| Minor Sixth (m6) | Major Sixth (M6) | Minor Seventh (m7) | Major Seventh (M7) |

Augmented and diminished intervals

If an interval is a semitone larger than a perfect or a major interval, it is called **augmented**. An interval that is a semitone smaller than a perfect or a minor interval is called **diminished**.

Augmented and diminished intervals

Augmented Prime   Diminished Second   Augmented Third   Diminished Sixth

Augmented Seventh   Diminished Octave   Augmented Fourth   Diminished Fifth

A diminished fifth and an augmented fourth are both six semitones (or three whole tones) so another term for this interval is a tritone.

Consonance and dissonance

Notes that sound good together when played at the same time are called **consonant**.

Notes that are **dissonant** can sound harsh or unpleasant when played at the same time. Or they may feel 'unstable'; if you hear a chord with a dissonance in it, you may feel that the music is pulling you towards the chord that **resolves** the dissonance. In music, certain combinations are consonant and others dissonant. Consonance and dissonance can refer to both chords and intervals.

The simple intervals that are considered to be **consonant** are the minor third, major third, perfect fourth, perfect fifth, minor sixth, major sixth, and the octave. Chords that contain only these intervals are considered to be 'stable', restful chords that don't need to be resolved.

The intervals considered to be **dissonant** are the minor second, the major second, the minor seventh, the major seventh, and particularly the tritone. These intervals are all considered to be tension-producing. In tonal music, chords containing dissonances are considered 'unstable'; when we hear them, we expect them to move on to a more stable chord. Moving from a dissonance to the consonance that is expected to follow it is called **resolution**.

The pattern of tension and release created by resolved dissonances is part of what makes a piece of music exciting and interesting.

Resolving dissonances

Rhythm

- The term **rhythm** as used by musicians can refer to many things. It can mean the basic, repetitive pulse of the music or a rhythmic pattern that is repeated throughout the music. It can also refer to the pattern of note values.
- The **beat** is the steady pulse in the music. Anything that happens at the same time as a strong pulse is 'on the beat'; anything that happens at any other time is 'off the beat' (syncopation).
- Measure or **bar**. Beats are grouped into measures or bars. The first beat is usually the strongest, and in most music, most of the bars have the same number of beats. This sets up a basic rhythm in the pulse of the music.
- **Syncopation** occurs when a strong note happens either on a weak beat or off the beat.

Some words to describe rhythmic features in a Listening Paper question:

• syncopated	• waltz-like
• dotted	• triplet
• complex	• free rhythm
• simple	• rubato
• strict/steady	• back beat
• polyrhythm	• hemiola.
• ostinato	

Time signatures

The **time signature** tells you the metre of the music by defining both the number of beats in a bar and the type of note value (minims, crotchets, quavers) that fills one beat.

The **metre** of a piece of music is its basic **pulse**; the time signature is the symbol that tells you the metre of the piece.

Beats and measures

In most music, things tend to happen right at the beginning of each beat. This is called being on the **downbeat**.

Clef, key signature and time signature

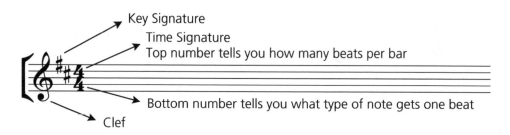

Key Signature

Time Signature

Top number tells you how many beats per bar

Bottom number tells you what type of note gets one beat

Clef

The **time signature** appears at the beginning of a piece of music, after the key signature. Only one time signature needs to be inserted in Questions 1–3 Melody Writing. Unlike the key signature, **do not** insert the time signature at the start of every stave/phrase, unless you are changing time signature (which there is no need for you to do).

Reading time signatures

Most time signatures contain two numbers. The top number tells you how many beats there are in a measure. The bottom number tells you what kind of note gets a beat. A few time signatures don't have to be written as numbers. 4/4 time is used so much that it is often called **common time**, written as a C.

Key signature

The **key signature** is a list of all the sharps and flats in the key that the music is in. The sharps or flats always appear in the **same order** in all key signatures.

Order of sharps and flats

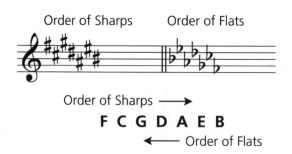

Order of Sharps   Order of Flats

Order of Sharps ⟶

F C G D A E B

⟵ Order of Flats

The key signature at the beginning of a musical stave lists the sharps or flats in the key. The key signature comes right after the clef symbols on particular lines or spaces, or some flat symbols. If there are no flats or sharps listed after the clef symbol, then the key signature is that all notes are **natural**.

If you do not know what key you are in, the key signature can help you find out.

If you are in a major key and if the key contains sharps, the name of the key (doh or tonic note) is one semitone higher than the last sharp in the key signature. If the key contains flats, the name of the key signature (doh or tonic note) is the name of the second-to-last flat in the key signature.

- Clef and key signature are the only symbols that must appear on every stave. The key signature tells you whether the note is sharp, flat or natural.
- In the diagram of the key signatures (below) you will see that sharps and flats are always added in the same order as keys get sharper or flatter. The order of flats and sharps, like the order of the keys themselves, follows a **circle of fifths**.

As part of your exam preparation, research **the circle of fifths** on the internet or in music theory books.

C major and F major

C major   F major

The only major keys that these **rules do not work for** are C major (no flats or sharps) and F major (one flat). It is easiest just to memorise the key signatures for these two very common keys.

Key signatures

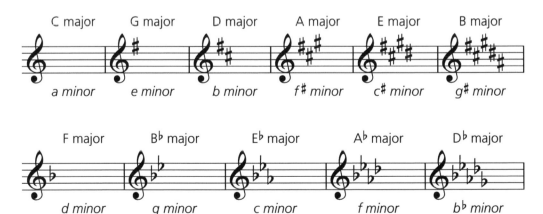

| C major | G major | D major | A major | E major | B major |

| a minor | e minor | b minor | f# minor | c# minor | g# minor |

| F major | Bb major | Eb major | Ab major | Db major |

| d minor | g minor | c minor | f minor | bb minor |

If the music is in a *minor* key, it will be in the **relative minor** of the major key for that key signature. If you cannot tell from the sound of the music whether you are in a major or minor key, the best clue is to look at the final chord and for any accidental in the given music.

A **relative minor** is always three semitones lower than its relative major.

The **harmonic minor scale** raises the seventh note of the scale by one half step, whether you are going up or down the scale.

In the **melodic minor scale**, the sixth and seventh notes of the scale are each raised by one half step when going up the scale and are flattened (naturalised) when going back down a scale. You must use this type of minor when composing melodies.

Melody

Words that describe the shape or contour of a melody:

- repeated notes
- stepwise motion
- interval leaps
- ascending
- descending
- triadic
- arpeggio
- countermelody
- descant.

A **melody** is a series of notes, one after another.

Melodic phrases

Melodies are often described as being made up of **phrases**. A melodic phrase is a group of notes that make sense together and express a definite melodic 'idea', but it takes more than one phrase to make a complete melody.

How do you spot a phrase in a melody? The melody usually pauses slightly at the end of each phrase (cadence point).

In vocal music, the musical phrases tend to follow the phrases and sentences of the text.

Harmony

Harmony is the relationship of any notes that happen at the same time.

Major and Minor chords

- The most commonly used triads form major chords and minor chords.
- All major and minor chords have an interval of a perfect fifth between the root and the fifth of the chord.
- If the interval between the root and the third of the chord is a major third the triad is a major chord.
- If the interval between the root and the third of the chord is a minor third the triad is a minor chord.

Major and minor chords

| In major chords, the third of the chord is a major third above the root. | In both major and minor chords, the fifth of the chord is a perfect fifth above the root. | In minor chords, the third of the chord is a minor third above the root. |

Augmented and Diminished chords

Because they don't contain a perfect fifth, augmented and diminished chords have an unsettled feeling and are normally used sparingly.

Here are some good **chord progressions** that you can use in Paper II:

- chord ii usually goes to V

    I – vi – IV – ii – V   or   I – IV – ii – V

    but chord V rarely goes to chord ii

- V can go to I, vi or IV
- chord vi usually goes either to chord IV or chord ii.

Harmonic textures

- **Implied harmony.** A melody all by itself (**monophony**) can have an implied harmony, even if no other notes are sounding at the same time. In melody writing (Questions 1–3 in the Composition Paper) construct a melody so that it strongly suggests a harmony that could accompany it.
- **Drones.** The simplest way to add harmony to a melody is to play it with drones. A drone is a note that changes rarely or not at all.
- **Parallel harmony** occurs when different lines in the music go up or down together (usually following the melody).
- **Homophony** is a texture of music in which there is one line that is obviously the melody. The rest of the notes are harmony and accompaniment.

Harmonic analysis

Harmonic analysis simply means understanding how a chord is related to the key and to the other chords in a piece of music.

- **Harmonic rhythm** refers to how often the chords change.
- **Diatonic** harmony stays in a particular major or minor key.
- **Chromatic** harmony includes notes and chords that are not in the key and so contains many accidentals.
- **Dissonance** refers to a note, chord or interval that does not fit into the triadic. A dissonance may sound surprising, jarring, even disagreeable.

Accompaniment

- All the parts of the music that are not melody are part of the **accompaniment**. This includes rhythmic parts, harmonies, the bass line, and chords.
- The **bass line** is the string of notes that are the lowest notes being sung or played. The bass line also often outlines the chord progression, and it is often the most noticeable line of the accompaniment.
- **Inner voices** are accompaniment parts that fill in the music between the melody (which is often the highest part) and the bass line.
- **Descant:** the melody is not always the highest line in the music. Attention is naturally drawn to high notes, so a part that is higher than the melody is sometimes given a special name such as 'descant'.

Basic triads in a major key

The most likely chords to show up in a key are the chords that you can make in that key without using accidentals. So these chords have both names and numbers that tell how they fit into the key. **The chords are numbered using Roman numerals from I to vii.**

- To find all the basic chords in a key, build a simple triad (in the key) on each note of the scale. You'll find that although the chords change from one key to the next, the **pattern** of major and minor chords is always the same.
- Capital roman numerals are used for major chords and small roman numerals for minor chords.
- In a major key, the chords built on the first, fourth, and fifth degrees of the scale are always **major chords** (I, IV, and V). The chords built on the second, third, and sixth degrees of the scale are always **minor chords** (ii, iii, and vi).

The chord built on the seventh degree of the scale is a **diminished chord**.

A HIERARCHY OF CHORDS

In most music, the most common chord is I. It is the tonal centre of the music. IV and V (or V7) are also likely to be very common.

Naming harmonic relationships

In classical music another set of names for chords (and their harmonic relationships) and degrees of the scale is commonly used.

<table>
<tr><td>I = tonic</td><td>V = dominant</td></tr>
<tr><td>ii = supertonic</td><td>vi = submediant</td></tr>
<tr><td>iii = mediant</td><td>vii = leading note</td></tr>
<tr><td>IV = subdominant</td><td></td></tr>
</table>

Modulation

Sometimes a piece of music moves into a new key. This is called modulation. It is very common in traditional classical music; longer movements almost always spend at least some time in a different key (usually a closely related key such as the *dominant* or the *relative minor* or *relative major*).

Triads in root position

Chords in root position are the most basic way to write a triad. In root position, the root, which is the note that names the chord, is the lowest note. The simplest way to write a triad is as a stack of thirds, in root position.

First and second inversions

Three triads of C major

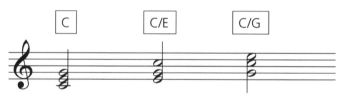

3 Triads of C major

If the third of the chord is the lowest note, the chord is in first inversion. If the fifth of the chord is the lowest note, the chord is in second inversion. It does not matter how far away the higher notes are, or how many of each note there are, all that matters is which note is lowest.

- C is a chord I of C and has C as its first lowest note (root position chord).
- C/E is a chord Ib of C with E as its first lowest note (first inversion). Do not overuse this type of chord as it is a weaker-sounding chord than a root position chord, but it does work very well in an ascending or descending progression: C, G/b, am, G, dm/f, G7, C.
- C/G is a chord Ic of C with G as its first lowest note (second inversion). This type of second inversion chord only works well at a Ic – V – I cadence point.

Treble clef and bass clef

Treble clef and bass clef

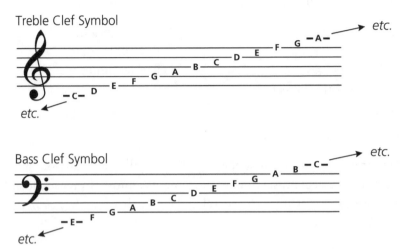

The clef symbol on a music stave tells you which pitches belong on the lines and spaces of that stave.

The first symbol that appears at the beginning of every stave is a clef symbol. It tells you which note (A, B, C, D, E, F or G) goes on each line or space. The other notes are arranged on the stave so that the next letter is always on the next higher line or space.

Alto clef and tenor clef

Most music these days is written in either bass clef or treble clef, but some music is written in the **alto** or tenor clef. Whatever line it centres on is middle C. Music is easier to read and write if most of the notes fall on the stave and few ledger lines have to be used. Instruments with ranges that do not fall comfortably into either bass or treble clef may use a C clef or may be transposing instruments.

A very small '8' at the bottom of the treble clef symbol means that the notes should sound one octave lower than they are written.

Triads

C Major Triads

C	dm	em	F	G⁷	am	bdim

I   ii   iii   IV   V⁷   vi   vii

G Major Triads

G	am	bm	C	D⁷	em	f#dim

I   ii   iii   IV   V⁷   vi   vii

D Major Triads

D	em	f#m	G	A⁷	bm	c#dim

I   ii   iii   IV   V⁷   vi   vii

A Major Triads

A	bm	c#m	D	E⁷	f#m	g#dim

I   ii   iii   IV   V⁷   vi   vii

E Major Triads

E	f#m	g#m	A	B⁷	c#m	d#dim

I   ii   iii   IV   V⁷   vi   vii

F Major Triads

F	gm	am	B♭	C⁷	dm	edim

I   ii   iii   IV   V⁷   vi   vii

B♭ Major Triads

B♭	cm	dm	E♭	F⁷	gm	adim

I   ii   iii   IV   V⁷   vi   vii

E♭ Major Triads

E♭	fm	gm	A♭	B♭⁷	cm	ddim

I   ii   iii   IV   V⁷   vi   vii

3 Set Works A

aims
● To gain a deeper understanding of the Set Works in group A, so that you can approach Set Works questions with confidence.

exam focus

TO BE EXAMINED IN 2017–2019

● J. S. Bach, Cantata BWV 78, 'Jesu, der du meine Seele' (1724)

● P. I. Tchaikovsky, *Romeo and Juliet* Fantasy Overture (1880)

● Gerald Barry, Piano Quartet No. 1 (1992)

● Queen, 'Bohemian Rhapsody' (1975)

Quick revision – Set Works A

Work	Movement/ Section	Time Signature	Key Signature	Style	Tempo
J.S. Bach (1685–1750) Cantata BWV 78 'Jesu, der du meine Seele'	Chorus SATB	3/4	g minor	Baroque sacred cantata for the fourteenth Sunday after Trinity, based on text by Johann Rist	No tempo markings
	Aria (Duet) Soprano and Alto	C	B♭ major		
	Recitativo Tenor	C	g minor/C		
	Aria Tenor	6/8	g minor		
	Recitativo Bass	C	E♭ major/ f minor		Vivace Adagio Andante
	Aria Bass	C	c minor		No tempo markings
	Chorale Chorus SATB	C	g minor; ends in G major		

Work	Movement/ Section	Time Signature	Key Signature	Style	Tempo
P.I. Tchaikovsky (1840–93) *Romeo and Juliet*	Introduction	C	f# minor f minor e minor b minor	Romantic symphonic fantasy overture	Andante non tasto quasi moderato
	Exposition		b minor Db major		Allegro guisto
	Development		f# minor g minor b minor		Allegro guisto
	Recapitulation		b minor D major b minor		Allegro guisto
	Coda		B major		Moderato assai
Queen 'Bohemian Rhapsody'	Intro	4/4 5/4	Bb major	Pop close-harmony style	Slowly
	Song	4/4 2/4	Bb major Eb major	Rock ballad	Slowly
	Opera	4/4 2/4	A major Ab major Eb major	Pastiche – popular operatic section	Twice as fast
	Song	4/4 2/4	Eb major	Rock style	Twice as fast
	Coda	4/4	Ends in F	Rock style	Tempo 1
Gerald Barry Piano Quartet No. 1	A *Sí Bheag, Sí Mhór*	3/4 4/4		Contemporary classical piano quartet with some trad Irish influences	♩. = 108
	B	3/4, 3/8,4/4, 2/4, 2/8, 5/8, 3/16			♩. = 72 ♩ = 80 ♩. (B2)
	C	3/4, 3/8, 2/8, 3/16, 2/4, 4/4			From ♪ = 58 to ♪ = 168

Work	Movement/ Section	Time Signature	Key Signature	Style	Tempo
Gerald Barry Piano Quartet No. 1	D	1/8, 3/16, 2/8, 3/8, 5/16, 3/4, 4/4, 2/4			♩ = 126 wild!
	E	3/4, 3/8, 2/8, 3/16, 4/4, 2/4, 2/8			♩ = 138 (E2)
	F	3/2, 3/4, 4/2, 3/8, 2/2			♩ = 138
	G	2/8, 3/16, 3/8, 2/4, 1/4,			♩ = 126
	H *Lord Mayo's Delight*	2/2, 3/4, 3/2, 3/8			𝅗𝅥 = 104

Instruments used in Set Works A

Composer	Vocal	Strings	Woodwind Brass	Brass	Percussion	Keyboard/ Other
Bach	✔	✔	✔	✔		✔
Tchaikovsky		✔	✔	✔	✔	
Queen	✔				✔	✔
Barry		✔				✔

J.S. Bach: 'Jesu, der du meine Seele' (Cantata BWV 78)

You should be able to:

- identify themes and movements from a listening or written extract
- identify instruments and voices in each movement from a listening or written extract
- understand the compositional and instrumental/vocal techniques used by Bach in this cantata
- understand the form, textures and harmonies used in each movement
- understand how Bach sets the text musically and what the text means
- understand the word setting (syllabic/melismatic).

OVERVIEW

- This cantata is a product of Bach's **Leipzig period**. It was written for the fourteenth Sunday after Trinity.
- It was at Leipzig, between 1723 and 1744, that Bach developed and perfected this form of the chorale cantata.
- The spirit of this form is that the entire chorale (hymn tune) becomes the basis of the cantata.
- The theme of this cantata is **consolation**.
- It is one of the best-known Bach cantatas and was one of Felix Mendelssohn's favourite cantatas.

Glossary

Aria: A song for soloist or duet.
Binary form: A B.
Canon: Strict imitation.
Cantata: A sacred or secular work composed for soloists, chorus and orchestra.
Chaconne theme: Where the theme begins in the bass and it continues in other instruments/voices.
Chorale: Choral or instrumental music based on a hymn tune.

Continuo: More than one instrument playing the accompaniment or bass line.
Da capo: An instruction to go back to the start and finish at *Fine*.
Figured bass: Notes underneath the bass line which indicate which notes the organ/harpsichord player plays. For example, if G is in the bass and 5/3 is written underneath the third and fifth notes over G will be played and so the chord will be G, B, D.

Homophonic: One line of melody with accompaniment.
Monophonic: One line of melody without accompaniment.
Polyphonic: Two or more lines of melody together.
Recitative: Speech-like song (narrating a story through song). There are two types of recitative: *recitative secco*, in which the accompaniment is sparse and chordal; and *recitative accompagnata*, in which the accompaniment is more complex and there is a thicker texture (more instruments).
Ritornello form: A theme is repeated over and over e.g. A B A C A D A B A.
Sequence: An idea repeated up or down a note.
Ternary form: A B A.
Word-painting: Something is described through music.

VOICE PARTS

- Soprano: high female voice.
- Alto: low female voice.
- Tenor: high male voice.
- Bass: low male voice.

Bach Cantata BWV 78 Movement/Voices	Instruments
Chorus SATB	2 violins, viola, cello (as part of continuo), flute, 2 oboes, continuo (harpsichord), horn (doubling soprano line)
Aria Duet Soprano and alto soloists	continuo (organ and cello) with double bass
Recitativo Tenor solo	continuo (organ or harpsichord and cello)
Aria Tenor solo	flute and continuo
Recitativo Bass solo	(accompanied recitative) 2 violins, viola and continuo
Aria Bass solo	oboe, 2 violins, viola and continuo
Chorale SATB chorus	Tutti doubling the vocal lines: S — flute, oboe I, violin I, horn A — oboe II, violin II T — viola B — continuo

Analysis of Cantata BWV 78

Movement 1

Text

'Jesus, you are my soul. Through your bitter death you powerfully saved me from the devil's wicked hell and the serious misery of my soul. And through your pleasant word you let me know this. You are now, oh Lord, my redemption.'

- Form: Ritornello form.
- Key: G minor. However, based on modulations in the Chorale: g minor – D – F – B flat – g minor.
- Three ideas/themes: 1a, 1b and 1c.

Theme 1a

Theme 1b

Theme 1c

FEATURES

- Polyphonic/contrapuntal texture
- Melisma on 'heraus' (away)
- Sequences
- Ornamentation
- Chromaticism
- Inversion (Ib)
- Word-painting (heraus), Ib downward chromatic scale suggesting suffering and descent into hell.

TEXTURE

- The cantata opens with a magnificent chorale-fantasia; a profoundly expressive lament. Along with the chorale (hymn tune) sung in the soprano voice, its basic material is provided by a chromatically descending theme four bars in length (theme 1b).

- This recurring theme gives the movement the form of a chaconne or passacaglia. This is a set of continuous variations on the chromatic descending 'ground bass'. The descending chromatic theme expresses the great pain, anguish and suffering of Christ.

- This first movement starts with alternating orchestral (theme 1a) and canonic and melismatic choral passages, and reaches a climax in which the tutti orchestra and chorus play and sing in complex polyphony.

- In the 144 bars of the first movement there are 27 chaconne repetitions, two of which are in inversion. It appears several times in the highest soprano part and in other keys (subdominant or dominant).

- The chaconne repetitions occur in sequence 22 times. There are stretto-like entries before the cantus firmus (chorale–hymn tune, in the soprano part) appears.

Movement 2: Aria Duet

Text

'You hurry with weak, but purposeful steps, oh Jesus, oh Master to help you. You search faithfully for the ill and disorientated. Oh hear. Oh hear. Oh hear how we raise our voices to pray for your help. Your merciful countenance be welcome to us.'

- **Form:** Da capo aria (ternary) with the first instrumental introduction, and then vocal theme returning several times (ritornello-like). A B A.
- **Key:** B flat major but modulates to g minor, c minor, d minor and D major.
- Soprano and alto soloists.
- **Two themes:** 2a and 2b.

Theme 2a

Theme 2b

FEATURES

- **Melisma** on 'eilen' (to hurry)
- **Word-painting** on 'eilen', 'Oh, Jesu' and 'zu dir'
- Walking bass
- Canon/imitative writing
- Parallel writing
- Polyphonic/**contrapuntal** texture.

TEXTURE

- Mainly **polyphonic**
- The second movement, a duet for soprano and alto, is melodically one of the most enchanting movements written by Bach.
- Bach uses **word-painting** in the opening line in the continuo instruments. 'We hasten with failing but diligent paces' is suggested by the optimistic, bouncing, quaver theme (theme 2a).
- The mood of this duet is a complete **contrast** to the slowly drooping figure of the first movement.
- The long, flowing, melismatic melodies of the A section contrast strongly with the short, punctuated words ('Ach! Hore, wie wir') in the B section. Imitation and sequential melodies are employed throughout.
- Bach personally marked the instrumental parts 'piano' whenever the voices enter. These unambiguous expression markings were an unusual feature of Baroque composition.

The following two recitatives (Movements 3 and 5) paint a picture of the sinfulness of man. Compared with these, the tenor and bass arias (Movements 4 and 6) are elegant and cheerful in mood: the tenor aria with its sustained joyful flute **obligato**, and finally the serene bass aria with its optimistic **concertante** style.

Movement 3: Tenor – Recitative Secco

Text

'Oh! I am a child of my sins. Oh! I wander all around. The scab of my sins which you can find all over me won't leave me in this mortality. My will aspires for the evil, though my soul cries 'Ah who will release me?' But to force flesh and blood and do the good is far beyond my strength. If I don't want to deny the harm, then I can count how many times I failed. Thus now, I take the pain and torture of my sins and the burden of my sorrows – if I didn't it would feel so unbearable – and deliver them with sighs, to you, Jesus. Don't count the misdeeds, Lord, which made you angry.'

- Recitative secco (secco means dry) – the vocalist and the continuo only.
- Form: Structure comes from the text (syllabic setting apart from the final three bars).
- Key: Use of unresolved diminished chords keeps the listener on edge, as there is no tonal centre. The final bar ends in a perfect cadence on the note C.

FEATURES

- Homophonic texture
- Syllabic writing
- Melisma on one word – 'zurnet' (anger)
- Pedal notes
- Ornament at end of movement (mordent)
- The mood is dramatised by the large interval jumps in the tenor voice and the great emphasis on the words of the text.

Movement 4: Tenor Aria

Text

'Your blood, which crosses out my guilt, makes my heart light again and cleans me, cleans me. If the ruler of hell calls me to fight Jesus, stand by my side so that I will be brave.'

- Form: Ritornello-like (flute and continuo introduction, interludes and coda) and ternary type form – A, B1, B2 voice.
- Key: G minor but with modulations to B♭ major and c minor.

FEATURES

- Homophonic texture: flute and continuo; polyphonic texture: flute, tenor and continuo
- Ornamentation and scale passages on flute
- Octave leaps/wide intervals on 'beherzt' (brave)
- Sequences
- Pedal notes
- Word-painting: 'beherzt' (brave), 'streite' (conflict), 'macht mir das Herze wieder leicht' (makes my heart light again).

Movement 5: Bass – Recitative Accompagnato

Text

'The wounds, nails, crown and grave; the thumps given to the Saviour there are now a sign of his victory and can give me new strength. If a dreadful judge announces the curse for the damned, you change it with your blessing. No pain and no torture can touch me because my Saviour knows them; and thus your heart burns with love for me, I lay down everything that is mine before you. This, my heart mingled up with grief – if your precious blood is sprinkled, is spilled on the cross – I give it now to you, oh Lord Jesus Christ.'

- Form: Arioso-style recitative (more melodic than declamatory style).
- Key: E♭ major with modulations to g minor, A♭ major and f minor.

FEATURES

- Texture: Mainly homophonic with a more contrapuntal texture in the Andante section (voice against strings and continuo)
- Rich in chromaticism
- Ornamentation
- Syllabic and melismatic text setting
- Pedal notes
- Wide interval jumps, which increase the dramatic and expressive power of the words. Also many sudden changes in tempo: *vivace – adagio – andante*. The indication *con ardore* (in the *vivace* section) increases the dramatic effect.

Movement 6: Bass Aria

Text

'You will appease my conscience if I am longing for revenge, because your word is promising hope for me. If Christians believe in you, no enemy in eternity can steal them out of your hands.'

- **Form:** Da capo aria (ternary form – A, B, A1) with ritornello-like oboe and string interludes.
- **Key:** C minor including modulations to g minor and f minor.

FEATURES

- **Homophonic** texture: oboe, strings and continuo; **polyphonic** texture: bass against countermelody oboe with continuo and strings
- Two main themes: 6a and 6b
- Ornamentation
- Sequences
- **Terraced dynamics** (*forte* or *piano*) can be seen throughout this movement.
- Word-painting: 'hoffnung' (hope), 'rauben' (taken), 'ewigkeit' (forever)
- Melisma
- Pedal note.

Movement 7: Chorale

Text

'Lord, I believe, therefore help me in my weakness. And don't let me give up hope. You can make me stronger when sin and death attack me; I will trust in your grace until I see you after the fight, joyful in eternity.'

- Finally, the hymn tune (**chorale**) is heard in its unadorned setting (homophonic) by the SATB chorus and tutti orchestra.
- **Key:** G minor but ending in a **tierce de picardie** in G major.
- Cadences every two bars: perfect (bar 2); imperfect (bar 4); perfect (bar 6); imperfect (bar 8); perfect into F major (bar 10); perfect into B♭ major (bar 12); imperfect (in tonic bar 14); and perfect into tonic major, G major (tierce de picardie) in final bar 16.

Tchaikovsky: *Romeo and Juliet* Fantasy Overture

Listen to many different versions of this piece as part of your exam preparation. Different interpretations of the music have brought about different recordings, with great variations in tempo, emphasis and style. There is even a pop-like version available in the iTunes store! You should also watch a DVD of *Romeo and Juliet*, so that you understand the story behind the music. Try Franco Zeffirelli's 1968 version or Baz Luhrmann's 1996 version.

Tschaikowsky

You should be able to:

- understand sonata form
- identify instrumentation
- explain the style and genre
- describe texture
- define the historical context
- describe characteristics of Romantic music
- identify key signatures and tonality of sections and themes
- understand tempo, rhythmic and melodic features
- explain cadence points
- describe dynamic contrasts between sections
- explain instrumental techniques, such as pizzicato, drum roll, etc.

Tchaikovsky's Romantic compositional style

- Tchaikovsky epitomised the Romantic era. Like many Romantic composers, he used dramatic **programme** music for the basis of his major works.
- His music combines dramatic intensity, emotional expressiveness and his love for Russian folk music and dance.
- He was an excellent orchestrator who chose **unusual instrument pairings** (e.g. cor anglais and viola).
- **Rushing semiquavers on strings** feature in his music.
- He used ascending scales and the occasional loud cymbal crash at climax points.

- Antiphonal blocks of wind/brass against strings occur.
- Long, winding melodies are present.
- Repeated rhythmic fragments feature. This shows an influence from the Classical style developed by Beethoven.
- Long *crescendi* build up musical tension.
- Extreme dynamic contrasts occur within pieces.

SONATA FORM

Exposition

- The exposition sets forth the themes. There are two distinct groupings: Subject I and Subject II.
- SII will be in contrast to SI. SII is often more lyrical and can be in a different key.
- Much other material, including other themes, may appear between and after SI and SII.
- A closing section is called a codetta.

Development

- Here the composer experiments with one or more of the themes from the exposition.
- Themes may be played on different instruments, made faster or slower, louder or softer. They are usually played in different keys, fragmented and tossed around the orchestra, often in insistent repetitions of the same tiny phrase or motif.
- The development is usually tense and dramatic.

Recapitulation

- This is essentially a repeat of the exposition, but can be very different, with themes omitted and new ones added.
- Usually more confident in style than the exposition.
- A coda or ending piece is used.

Instruments used in *Romeo and Juliet*

- Full symphony orchestra used throughout
- Woodwind: piccolo, two flutes, two oboes, two clarinets in A, cor anglais, two bassoons
- Brass: four horns in F, two trumpets in E, two trombones, bass trombone, tuba
- Percussion: three timpani, cymbals, bass drum
- Strings: violins I, violins II, violas, cellos, double basses and harp.

Transposing Instruments

- **Clarinet in A** sounds a minor third lower than written
- **Cor anglais** sounds a perfect fifth lower than written
- **Double bass** sounds an octave lower than written
- **Horn in F** sounds a perfect fifth lower than written
- **Piccolo** sounds an octave higher than written
- **Trumpet in E** sounds a major third higher than written.

OVERVIEW

- Tchaikovsky's *Romeo and Juliet* Fantasy Overture is a piece of **programme music**. Tchaikovsky's objective was to create the general impression of Shakespeare's play.
- Programme music describes something, e.g. a scene or a story.
- Tchaikovsky dedicated the *Romeo and Juliet* Fantasy Overture to Balakirev.
- It was first performed in Moscow in 1870 and was not successful. Tchaikovsky then modified the work and this version was first performed in 1880.
- Though there are only 522 bars in the overture, the time difference between recordings can be as much as three to four minutes. Listen to a variety of recordings and see which you prefer. Some can be very Romantic and texturally dense while others can be fast, light and Classical in performance.

exam focus

Use your full score to copy main themes and motifs from all of your Set Works into your music manuscript. It may be tedious work but it really helps you to become more meticulous at music notation.

Glossary

A due (a2): Two instruments play the same line of music.
Arco: With the bow. (Since this the normal way to play stringed instruments, it is best not to list this as a technical feature in a Leaving Certificate Music exam answer.)
Allegro: Fast.
Allegro guisto: Fast and steady.
Andante non tanto quasi moderato: Literally 'at a walking pace, not too much, semi-moderately'.
Con sordini: With mute.
Div.: Divided.
Dolce: Sweetly.

Dolce ma sensibile: Sweetly but sensitively.
Espress.: Expressively.
Marc.: Marcato (accented).
Moderato assai: Extremely moderate.
Molto meno mosso: Not as much.
Pizz.: Pizzicato (plucked).
Poco a poco string(endo) accel(erando): Little by little getting faster and louder.
Sempre: Always.
Senza sordini: Without mute.
String(endo) al …: Faster and louder to …
Unis.: Unison.
***Note: There is no tremolo in the strings.**

Analysis of *Romeo and Juliet* Fantasy Overture

Introduction

- Bars 1–111.
- The main theme is the **Friar Laurence** theme, sometimes called the **Ecclesiastical** theme.

Romeo & Juliet Friar Laurence theme

- Many other smaller melodic and rhythmic **motifs** occur in this very long and slow introduction.
- The theme is in **two parts**: a *chorale* progression of woodwind chords that are supposed to represent Friar Laurence, and a following ascending and descending pattern in the strings and horns, with winds later.
- The theme is repeated down a semitone but two octaves higher in the flutes and oboes, in f minor, over pizzicato strings.
- **Key:** F sharp minor (the tonic of the overall overture is b minor).
- **Metre:** common time (4/4).
- Texture: **Homophonic chorale.**
- The theme is played **three times** in the introduction. First time: clarinets and bassoons. Second time: flute, clarinet and oboe play melody and pizzicato strings accompany. Third time: thicker texture, more instruments join in, more dynamics, arpeggios on harp and timpani all combined to create an unsettled mood.

- **Main instruments:** two clarinets and two bassoons introduce the theme. All of the instruments are involved at some stage in the introduction.

- **Arpeggi on the harp** are a dominant feature also.

- **Mood:** Tension and anticipation increasing and decreasing throughout by use of shifting block instrumentation, pedal notes, timpani rolls, chromatic variation of the theme and counterpoint and contrary motion in the string accompaniment.

Exposition

- Bars 112–272.

- There are many different names for all the different themes and motifs in this work. Do not get confused by them. Once you are able to **describe the theme and its musical characteristics** that is all that is needed.

- Within the exposition there are two distinct groupings of main themes: **Subject I** group and **Subject II** group. There is an obvious difference between the first and second subjects, as is the case in most sonata form movements. SI is rhythmic and strong, while SII is melodic, lyrical and legato.

Subject I: Strife theme

- **Key:** SI is in g minor.

- The first theme, in full orchestra, is supposed to represent the Montague–Capulet feud. This theme can be broken down further into a **six motifs** or sections, the first four being developed throughout the development and recapitulation sections.

- **Motifs of SI:** short melodic fragments that Tchaikovsky develops throughout the exposition, development and recapitulation. **The second beat of bar 112** (the three repeated F sharps) is a motif that Tchaikovsky uses throughout the development and recapitulation sections.

Allegro giusto

- **SIb (bars 115–118):** Ascending string scale passage in semiquavers (also known as 'motif e').

- **SIc (bars 118–120):** Semitone motif ('motif f') is the quaver semitone motif heard first in the wind and horns in bars 118 and 119.

- **SId (bars 122–126):** Ascending repeated three-note sequential motif, usually heard in strings alternating (antiphonal) with woodwind. This is also known as the 'link theme' or 'motif g'.

- **SIe (bars 126–135):** A rhythmically altered version of the first subject is played in canon by the cellos and double basses, and woodwind instruments (piccolo, flute and clarinet). Violins I and violins II play alternating swirling scale passages and this builds tension, which is punctuated by loud brass, woodwind and percussion with syncopated accents.

FEATURES

- Texture: mainly **homophonic**.
- Main **instruments**: tutti. Tchaikovsky's orchestration uses timbre (instrumental sound colour) in blocks of sound: sequences of strings against woodwind, etc.
- Mood: formidable and powerful.
- Use of a chain of **dominant sevenths**.
- Vibrant, full texture in b minor by the full orchestra.
- **Rushing scale passages** in the strings (a common Tchaikovsky string orchestration).
- An array of developed fragmented **motifs**, quaver, semiquaver and dotted rhythms and sequential scale passages are utilised by Tchaikovsky to hasten the music towards a *fortissimo* **climax**.
- What happens instead is a release of tension, a sudden *diminuendo*, and a transition (developing the rising three-note motif) leading to an **unusual modulation** to D flat (instead of to D major, the relative major of b minor) and the introduction of a the SII melodies (Love theme).
- The transitions are played above an A note (dominant) pedal and seem to be predicting the Love theme in D major. (We finally get the Love theme in D major in the recapitulation.)

Subject II: Love theme

- **SIIa (bars 184–192):** Love theme in D flat major (not D major, the relative major to b minor). Cor anglais and muted (con *sordini*) violas play first version with pizzicato lower strings and syncopated horn. The theme is later played by flutes and oboes with *tutti* accompaniment and descending, sequential two-note countermelody (polyphonic) in horns.

- **SIIb (bars 192–212):** Second part of the Love theme is played *pp* by *divisi* strings *con sordini*. In the recapitulation, SIIb is heard before SIIa is heard!

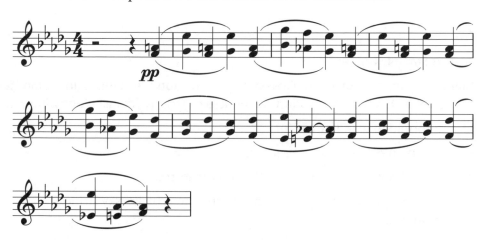

- **Motif *b* (bars 205–212)** is developed sequentially throughout this section.

FEATURES

- There are two second subject themes: the expressive and lyrical Love theme proper (Subject IIa) in bars 184–192, the universally renowned melody; and the shimmering muted string (diminished fifth) arpeggio figure (SIIb) in bars 192–212.
- Key: D flat major. Instead of D major, the relative major, we hear SII in D major in the recapitulation.
- Texture: homophonic (first rendition); polyphonic (second rendition – with the descending 'sighing' countermelody motif on the French horns).
- Orchestration: First time: cor anglais and muted violas; second time: flute and oboe; third time: flute, oboes and clarinets. Strings predominately used as an accompaniment (but used for melody in recapitulation).
- The eight-bar Love theme is accompanied by pizzicato cellos and double basses with French horns playing syncopated chords.
- Sequential development of the Love theme is used.
- A dominant pedal in the lower strings and bassoons helps the harmonic suspensions and resolutions throughout this section.
- The flute and oboe ascending semiquaver scales leading to the reoccurrence of SII intensify the passionate sentiment that Tchaikovsky is trying to achieve.
- Rubato may be employed by the performers to give this theme a lush, romantic feel.
- The harp is again employed using descending alternating chord inversions.
- The lyrical mood peacefully dies away into silence. Tchaikovsky often ends his expositions in this way so that huge contrast with the development can be achieved.
- A viola F natural brings the exposition to a close.

Development

- Bars 273–352.
- The development is based on the Friar Laurence theme and fragments of the Strife theme (SI).
- The development section is then easily identifiable because the mood again becomes tense and violent.
- Of the three main themes, SIIa (the Love theme) is not used in this development section.
- The key signature of b minor has vanished and we are left sensing only a vague tonal centre.
- SI motifs fragment into urgent murmur in the strings and the sequential patterns of the Friar Laurence theme are blazed out on the four horns. The brass and woodwind

woodwind question each other in an antiphonal manner over syncopated string accompaniment.

- The music reaches the first real *fortissimo* climax with a cymbal crash, and the Friar Laurence theme is then blasted by the **two trumpets** over a rhythmic ostinato taken from the opening of SI.

- The key of b minor is finally established in the rushing semiquaver string scales that lead directly to the recapitulation.

Recapitulation

- Bars 353–484.

- Key: B minor.

- Themes are not all in the same order as before. Much **classical-like development** of these original SI and SII themes occurs in this elongated section.

- You can tell you've reached the recapitulation because the SI theme is **played in full** (*tutti* and *ff*) for the first time since the beginning of the exposition.

- **The second section of the Love theme (SIIb) enters first** and is played by woodwind instead of violins.

- The lyrical Love theme melody (SIIa) comes second this time in the piccolo and strings with triplet accompaniment in the woodwind along with the descending sequential horn countermelody. It is very **lush and romantic** in mood.

- After the full statement of the Love theme, the mood turns **tense** as the music goes into the **minor** mode.

- The Strife theme (SIa) begins to re-emerge as the music leads into what really is a second development section within the recapitulation.

- Tutti orchestra unites to increase the tension as the **climax** to the entire overture is reached. The climax is marked *fff* (bar 473) and consists of fragments of the Strife and Love themes. It ends in dominant F sharp, timp roll with bassoons and lower strings also.

Coda (the Funeral)

- Bars 485–522 (end).

- Key: B major.

- Tempo: **Moderato assai** (rather moderate speed).

- The **Funeral** scene has a calm mood.

- **Triplet timpani ostinato rhythms** open the quiet Coda section in B major.

- The **Love theme** is played in the **minor** mode by bassoon, viola and cello, giving a sense of the final tragedy. It is followed by the full woodwind section playing Friar Laurence's **chorale**.

- A final serene rendition of the Love theme is heard high in the strings before the overture finishes with loud *tutti* syncopated tonic major chords over a timpani roll.

Gerald Barry: Piano Quartet No.1

OVERVIEW
Instruments

- piano
- violin
- viola
- cello.

Style

- It is in a contemporary, classical atonal idiom.
- Three Irish traditional melodies are used as the cornerstones of this distinct, sectional work.
- Nua Nós, a contemporary Irish ensemble, premiered it on 6 December 1992 in London.
- Only metronome markings are used for each section. Barry mixes 'mood' words and musical descriptions of how to play the music with the metronome figure in a very detailed and exacting manner, e.g. 'wild!', 'not slower!', 'with great verve and clarity', 'jauntily', 'subito!'
- There are twenty different indications of metronomic time in this work.

Score reading this work can be difficult because of the very fast tempos, changing pulses and contrapuntal textures. The work is very sectional and has distinct themes.

Here are a few helpful pointers:

- Mark off each section in your score to enable you to identify the following section if you get lost.
- On your score write in 'slow', 'moderate', 'fast', etc. over the changing metronome marks.
- Try to train your eye to score-read better by listening out for specific features or easily recognisable instrumental entries at certain points of the score.
- A blank score will not help your active listening!

Instrumental techniques

- Senza vibrato
- Piano clusters
- Harmonics
- Flautando
- Triplets
- Pedal.

Compositional techniques

- Canon
- Retrograde
- Inversion
- Polymetry
- Changing time signatures: over 330 changes!
- Transposition.

The three Irish tunes used as a basis for Gerald Barry's Piano Quartet No. 1 are:

- 'Sí Bheag Sí Mhór' [A]
- 'The Last Rose of Summer' [C]
- 'Lord Mayo's Delight' [H].

Glossary

Detaché: Detached.
Espressivo: Expressively.
Sim.: Play in a similar fashion.

Subito: Suddenly.
8ve: Play an octave higher (or lower, under the bass stave) than written.

Play note on open string

Pizzicato (plucked)

Harmonics

Form: unusual Rondo Form
A / B^1 /C^1 / C^2 / B^2 / C^3 / D^1 / D^2+B^3 / E / C^4 / C^5 / E^2+D^3 / C^6 / C7 / F+C^8 /C^9 / G / H

- **A, F, G** and **H** occur only once
- **B** occurs **three** times
- **C** occurs **nine** times
- **D** occurs **three** times
- **E** occurs **twice**.

Analysis of Barry's Piano Quartet No. 1

Section		Features	Instruments
A	Sí Bheag, Sí Mhór (C major!) Two parts	Four- and five-part canon at ♩ Inversion of Irish tune	Tutti Extremes in register in second part Heard once only
B1	'Village Band' Dissonances Changing metre	Three variations of this tune Open fifth accompaniment	Vln & Vla + Cello + Hand clusters on piano
C1	A flat tonality Senza vibrato Calm section, then suddenly violent	Irregular, jerky rhythms Contrapuntal texture	Vln, Vla, VC + Pno
C2	'Spirit of viol' playing in sixteenth-century style – two parts	Bigger melodic intervals than C1	Vla & VC + Vln
B2	B melody played five times	Three-part canon Contrasting texture and mood	Vln, Vla, VC + Pno (RH then LH)
C3	C melody played four times. Viol playing – atonal	Violin and cello homophonic and very dissonant	Vln, Vla, VC + Pno (fragments) violin descant superimposed
D1	New material – a minor	Rhythmically volatile – jazzy	Vla & VC only
D2+B3	D2 on violin and piano	B3 on viola, cello and piano (left hand)	Rhythmically distorted
E	E1 is the retrograde of D2	Four-part canon at ♪	Piano (LH) & Vln, Vla, VC
C4	Hommage à Horowitz	Piano octaves of C2	Solo piano
C5	Violin part of C3 played twice	Three-part canon	Vln, Vla, VC
E2+D3	E2 is retrograde of D with D also	Transposed into b♭ minor	D3 – VC and Pno E2 – Vln and Vla
C6	Shorter version of C5	Transposed Flautando	Vln, Vla, VC
C7	Sounds new but is inverted C music	Striding	Tutti
F+C8	Augmented C2 in Vla and VC	Polymetry: 2/2 v 3/4, etc.	F in the Vln – retrograde in the Pno
C9	Slowest C section music	Two octaves between parts	Vln, Vla, VC
G	Fragments telescoped together	First and last moments of each section	Tutti
H	Lord Mayo's Delight	Two- and three-part canons Heard once only	Vla & VC + Pno + Vln

Queen: 'Bohemian Rhapsody'

'Bohemian Rhapsody' was written by Freddie Mercury and appeared on the Queen album *A Night at the Opera* (1975). The band members were:

- Freddie Mercury: piano and vocals
- Brian May: lead guitar
- Roger Taylor: percussion
- John Deacon: bass guitar.

The single was released on 31 October 1975 and it held the number-one position for nine weeks in the UK. It was championed by DJ Kenny Everett on Capital Radio, and Freddie Mercury won his second Ivor Novello Award for the song, while the British Phonographic Industry awarded it Best Single of 1975. The 'Bohemian Rhapsody' video is considered to be the first real 'music video'.

You should be able to:

- describe the style of Queen as a rock band
- analyse the form, instrumentation, style and production of 'Bohemian Rhapsody'
- discuss the recording techniques and vocal techniques used in the making of the record
- examine the influence that 'Bohemian Rhapsody' has had since its release
- identify the chordal progressions, keys and modulations used throughout.

WHY IS 'BOHEMIAN RHAPSODY' SO POPULAR?

- Good studio and video production
- Catchy melody
- Diversity in musical styles
- Use of a non-standard song form
- Non-regular phrasing
- Limited use of repetition
- Rhythm: use of off-beat accents, tricky syncopation, triplets and unusual metre(s)
- Use of modulation

- Use of unusual chord progressions
- Harmonious melody and accompaniment
- Overall cohesion without being predictable
- Completely innovative in all respects
- Skilful performance, especially live (operatic section pre-recorded for live gigs)
- Good interplay between lyrics and music.

Styles used:
- Pop/ballad
- Rock
- Operatic.

Recording techniques used:
- Panning
- Overdubbing (vocal and instrumental)
- Flanged cymbals ('any way the wind blows'): this effect can only be achieved with a synthesiser.
- Multi-track recording
- Distortion (guitar interlude)
- Reverberation.

Vocal techniques:
- A capella singing (Introduction)
- Falsetto singing (Operatic section)
- Antiphonal singing, call and response (Operatic section)
- Four-part harmony (Introduction).

Guitar techniques (in Guitar interlude)
- Glissando bends
- Vibrato
- Riff
- Lick.

FORM

Introduction / Main song / Guitar interlude / Operatic section / Second song, Rock section / Recap and Coda.

- This six-minute song is a fusion of 1970s rock, pop and opera.
- Queen used to perform the song on stage without the Introduction, and the Opera section was played back from tape, providing a perfect opportunity for a light-show.
- The basic harmonies of the first phrase: gm7/D/C7/F7/B♭/B♭.
- Hardly any pop songs reached the level of complexity that can be found in the more sophisticated Queen songs.

Introduction

- Bars 1–15
- Key: B flat major
- Style: slow rock.

FEATURES

- Changing time signatures: 4/4 and 5/4
- Syncopation
- Repetition
- A *capella* singing (four-part close harmony vocals)
- Word-painting
- Flanged cymbal ('any way the wind blows')
- Panning
- Chromaticism (descending bass line)
- Texture: backing vocals, then piano accompaniment figure
- Overdubbing.

Main Song

- Bars 15–47
- There are two verses in the main song, so ensure that you are able to give two differences between Verse 1 and Verse 2.
- Key: B flat/E flat
- Style: **ballad style**
- Metre: 4/4, 2/4
- Texture: **homophonic.**

FEATURES

- **Word-painting** in Verse 1 with bell tree ('sends shivers down my spine')
- Accompaniment: developed broken chords on piano
- Descending **chromatic scale** in piano and bass guitar
- Syllabic word setting throughout
- Bass guitar glissando
- Bass rhythm changes to minim.

Verse 1	Verse 2
Piano, bass guitar	Piano, bass guitar, drums from beginning of Verse 2
Drums join in half way through verse	Backing vocals join in half way through verse
Solo voice	

Bridge after Verse 2 (Guitar interlude)

- Bars 47–55
- Key: E flat
- Style: heavy rock
- Metre: 4/4
- Orchestration: lead guitar solo (lick) with bass and drums.

FEATURES

- Bends
- Vibrato
- Glissando
- Guitar overdubs
- Distortion
- Syncopation
- Triplet rhythm
- Chromatic descending bass line doubled on bass guitar and piano left hand.

Operatic section

- Bars 55–95
- Key: A major, then A flat major
- Tempo: *l'istesso tempo*: new tempo's crotchet is the same as the old tempo's quaver, therefore it exactly doubles in speed. This is rather dramatic in style!
- Metre: 4/4, 2/4
- Instrumentation: piano.

FEATURES

- Falsetto singing
- Antiphonal singing/call and response
- Word-painting
- Panning
- Chromatisism
- Overdubbing
- Triplet rhythm
- Texture: homophonic and polyphonic
- Use of diminished chords
- Unexpected change of tempo, texture and key
- Guitars and drums enter before the next section, the hard rock riff, building up into a rich texture
- Rhythm section in triplets.

Second Song, Rock section

- Bars 96–122
- Key: E flat major
- Style: hard rock
- Metre: 12/8, 4/4
- Orchestration: lead guitar, bass guitar and drums; no piano.

FEATURES

- Melody: solo voice in triplet rhythm, very high, extended range
- Texture: rich, homophonic
- Distortion
- Syncopation
- Loudest section in song
- Overdubbed guitar tracks with heavy, distorted guitar licks
- Sudden D flat chord (flattened VII chord)
- Lead guitar lick uses modulating scale patterns
- Piano rejoins at bar 121 and the tempo slows.

Recap and Coda

- Bars 123–132
- Key: E flat, but ends on the chord of F major
- Style: slow rock
- Metre: 4/4
- Instrumentation: solo voice, overdubbed, panned guitars in imitation
- Backing vocals ('ooh') recall the first song; drums drop out
- Gong and piano end the piece
- In this section the tempo is freer (rubato) and the texture is more sparse.

HIGHER LEVEL QUESTION 1, 2007

An excerpt from the Cantata 'Jesu, der du meine Seele' by J.S. Bach.

The full excerpt will be played ONCE only. Sections A, B and C, taken from this excerpt, will then be played THREE times. There is a twenty second gap between each playing of the music in this question.

Section A, Bars 1–8

(i)   From which movement is this excerpt taken?

_____

(ii) Identify the woodwind instrument which plays the melody in this section.

_____

      Name two features of Baroque music that can be heard in this melody.

      1 _____   2 _____

(iii) Identify the cadence at X (bar 8). Do not use chord symbols or roman numerals.

Section B, Bars 17–26

Nun du wirst___ mein Ge - wis - sen - stil - len, so wi - der mich um Ra - - che, um Ra-che schreit ja, dei - ne Treu-e wird's-er - fül - len, weil mir dein Wort die Hoff - - - nung beut, weil mir - dein___ Wort die Hoff - - - - - nung, die Hoff-nung beut.

(i) Identify the type of voice heard in this section.

_____

(ii) In which bar are the strings (violins and violas) heard for the first time in this section?

_____

The rhythmic figure played by the strings in this bar is

(iii) Insert the four missing melody notes at Y on the score (bar 23).

Section C, Bars 26–53. There is no printed music for this section.

(i) Explain the term 'ritornello'.

_____

(ii) Describe Bach's specific use of ritornello in this section.

_____

_____

(iii) Identify two features of the vocal line in this section.

1 _____   2 _____

HL

(iv) Throughout this movement, the continuo reads from a bass line with figures underneath. Explain.

_____

_____

_____

_____

(25 marks)

4 Set Works B

aims
- To gain a deeper understanding of the Set Works in group B, so that you can approach Set Works questions with confidence.

exam focus

TO BE EXAMINED IN 2020–2023

- W. A. Mozart, Piano Concerto No. 23 in A, K488 (1798)
- Hector Berlioz, Symphonie Fantastique (1830)
- Raymond Deane, *Seachanges (with Danse Macabre)* (1993)
- The Beatles, *Sgt. Pepper's Lonely Hearts Club Band* (1967)

Quick revision – Set Works B

Work	Movement/ Section	Time Signature	Key Signature	Style	Tempo
Mozart (1756–91) **Piano Concerto No. 23, K488**	I	C	A major	Classical solo concerto	Allegro
	II	6/8	f# minor		Adagio
	III		A major		Allegro assai
Berlioz (1803–69) **Symphony Fantastique**	II *Un Bal* (*The Ball*); waltz	3/8	A major	Romantic symphonic programme music	Allegro non troppo
	IV *Marche au Supplice (March to the Scaffold)*		g minor (ends in G major)		Allegretto non troppo
The Beatles *Sgt. Pepper's Lonely Hearts Club Band*	'Sgt. Pepper's Lonely Hearts Club Band'	4/4	G major	Popular songs with instrumental accompaniment	Moderately slow, with a strong beat
	'She's Leaving Home'	3/4	E major		Moderate
	'When I'm Sixty-four'		C major		Steady 2 beat

Work	Movement/ Section	Time Signature	Key Signature	Style	Tempo
Deane (b. 1953) *Seachanges (with Danse Macabre)*	Section I	Many time signatures	No tonal key signature. Atonal, but based on three-note cell: G, A, C	Contemporary quintet for mixed ensemble	♩ = 80
	Section II	7/4			♩ = 120
	Section III	6/4 3/2			♩ = 80
	Section IV	7/8 7/4			♩ = 120
	Section V	6/4 3/2			♩ = 80
	Section VI	7/4			♩ = 120

Instruments used in Set Works B

Composer	Vocal	Strings	Woodwind	Brass	Percussion	Keyboard/ Other
Mozart		✔	✔	✔		✔
Berlioz		✔	✔	✔	✔	
The Beatles	✔	✔	✔	✔	✔	✔
Deane		✔	✔		✔	✔

Recognition of instruments is always tested in the Listening exam. Knowing what instruments are used in each section of each Set Work is a great foundation for Paper I. In the months before your exam, listen to all your Set Works at least **ten times** in your own revision time. It is the only way to fully understand each Set Work.

Mozart: Piano Concerto No. 23 in A Major K488

OVERVIEW

- The A major concerto (K488) was one of three piano concertos written during the winter of 1785–86, while Mozart was also at work on his opera *The Marriage of Figaro*.

- Mozart himself probably premiered it during March 1786.

- The concerto uses clarinets in place of oboes, and Mozart's emphasis on the woodwinds can be felt early in the movement. The pianist's role is a little subdued in the first movement, but there are some brilliant flashes in the cadenza.

- This concerto is set in the usual three-movement form. It is one of his most attractive works, contrasting a refined opening movement with a pathos-laden second movement and a bubbling, cheerful finale.

- The dialogue of the piano and orchestra cannot be reduced to a simple alternation of 'tutti' and 'solo' sections; the soloist engages in a constant exchange of ideas with smaller or larger groups from the ensemble.

- The concerto combines in its music a symphonic expression with the soloist's brilliance and wealth of ideas, all of which is set against the backdrop of a supremely clear-cut form.

- The key of f sharp minor (a romantic key), the tonic of the slow second movement, is extremely rare in Mozart's output – in fact, this is the only time it is used as the main key of any entire movement in all of Mozart's works.

You should know the following musical terms:

- **Alberti bass:** Broken-chord accompaniment in the bass.
- **Binary form:** A B.
- **Cadenza:** Solo passage where the musician can show off their skill and talent. It usually appears at the end of a piece.
- **Canon:** Imitation.

- Homophonic/polyphonic (counterpoint).
- Motif: Short musical idea that recurs in a piece of music. This idea can be developed.
- Pedal note.
- Rondo form: A B A C A D A.
- Solo concerto: A piece usually in three movements for a soloist and orchestra.
- Sonata form: Large scale ternary form. A – Exposition, B – Development and C – Recapitulation.
- Ternary form: A B A.

Instruments used

Strings	Woodwind	Brass	Keyboard
Violins I and II	1 flute (sounds a third lower than written)	2 horns in A (sound a third lower than written). These horns had no valves so could only play the harmonic series. Used mainly for filling out texture.	Piano (wooden framed piano). The range of dynamics would not be as great as today's instruments.
Violas	2 clarinets in A		
Cellos	2 bassoons		
Double basses (double the cello line at an octave below)	No oboes were used by Mozart in this orchestration: he favoured the clarinet's timbre and flexibility		

Glossary

Arco: With the bow.
Cadenza: A virtuosic, improvised section by the soloist.
Mordant: Turn.
Pizz.: Pizzicato (plucked).

Tr.: Trill.
Tutti: All instruments playing.
Zu 2: Same as a2; two instruments play in unison.

Form

- The opening movement is in the classical **sonata** form, involving a double exposition.
- The **adagio**, lyrical and extremely tender, is in three parts with the return of the opening section, and the finale follows a **rondo** pattern.

- At the outset, the slow movement is unusual in two ways. First, it is Mozart's first piano concerto slow movement to be labelled *Adagio*. (*Andante* or *Larghetto* are more common.) Second, Mozart wrote it in the key of f sharp minor, a 'romantic' key rarely found in his music.

Analysis

- Key: A major.
- Form: Sonata form.
- Number of bars: 313 (excluding cadenza).
- The first movement is set in a modified sonata form, as was typical of Classical concertos.
- Mozart uses a **double exposition**.
- The **trill** over a dominant seventh chord was the device used in classical concerto cadenzas for the soloist to signal to the orchestra their return.
- This cadenza tells us a great deal about Mozart the **improviser**: besides virtuosic passages, it also contains expressive, singing music, and expands on the concerto's thematic material in simple yet ingenious ways.
- Mozart refrains from always repeating material exactly, and keeps a feeling of **freshness** by allowing the pianist to embellish the main themes.

Active listening: themes

First movement

Themes in Mozart's Piano Concerto K488

Exposition	Piano Exposition	Codetta	Development	Recapitulation	Coda
SIa	SIa	Theme E	Use of Theme E	SIa	SIIb
SIb*	SIb			SIb	
SIIa	SIIa			SIIa	
SIIb	SIIb			SIIb	
	SIb			Theme E Cadenza	
Key: A	A–E	E	E, em, C, am, F, E–A	A	A

* SIb is *never* played in the piano part

Exposition

In Classical concerto sonata form there is typically a **double exposition**. This means that the main first and second subjects are presented by the orchestra alone, and then by the soloist. The orchestra's exposition presents both subjects in the tonic key.

The soloist begins their exposition in the tonic key with the first subject, but modulates for the second subject.

SI – First subject

- Key signature: A major
- Time signature: 4/4
- Strings open in the **tonic key**
- **8-bar structure**
- After eight bars, the **woodwinds** take up the same theme
- Ends with a repeated **perfect cadence**
- **Dotted rhythms** in the woodwind leave the music hanging in mid-air, preparing the way for the second subject.

SII(a) – Second subject

- Violins I
- Graceful

- **Chromatic movement**
- **Falling lines**
- Descending sequences
- **Repeated notes** accentuate the bass line
- Theme is restated with the flute and bassoon joining in.

SII(b)

- **Dialogue** between the strings and woodwind
- Dotted rhythms
- A major.

Piano entry

- Piano plays Subject I with left hand alberti bass accompaniment
- **Melodic** decoration
- Arpeggiated figures
- Fast scalic figures
- Modulation to the **dominant** (E major) finally happens when flute, bassoon and violin I play SII
- Piano **doubles it** in broken octaves
- Strings **imitate** the wind an octave higher
- Piano plays sparkling semiquaver runs
- Long **trills** are often used to emphasise important cadential points
- Original material is transposed into the **dominant** key.

A new theme appears in bar 143:

- E major
- Strings
- Suspended notes
- Dotted rhythm
- Syncopation.

Development

- This new 'development' material is developed and the sense of **tonality is destabilised.**
- Mozart makes great use of **textural contrast** here by juxtaposing legato winds with staccato strings in segments of two bars each.
- Mozart uses sequential and imitative development through numerous keys, the harmony following the **circle of fifths.**
- This involves both orchestra and soloist, and culminates in a dominant pedal, bring the tonality back to the **original tonic.**
- The piano uses arpeggiated and scalic figures to elaborate on the sustained harmonies in the orchestra.
- Canon between clarinet and flute – bar 170.
- Solo piano plays a **cadenza-like passage** which leads to the recapitulation.

Recapitulation

- Subject I
- A major
- Violin I and woodwind
- Piano enters with an **embellished** second half of the theme
- Grace notes, falling arpeggios and scales a tenth apart
- **Recapitulation** continues to be based on the soloist's version of the exposition
- Use of the **dominant pedal of E** is prevalent
- Soloist recalls the second subject, **transposed up a perfect 4th** into the tonic key of A major

- The **orchestra** takes over the theme as they did in the exposition
- The **soloist** again decorates this with broken RH octaves
- The piano alone plays a lengthy passage of virtuoso writing while the orchestra develops themes in an imitative manner similar to that in the development section
- The bass line slides chromatically from here to land on a tonic chord in second inversion, full of expectancy for the soloist to leap into a virtuosic **cadenza**
- Movement ends with **perfect cadences in the tonic.**

Adagio, second movement

- The second movement's dominating sentiment in many ways **foreshadows musical Romanticism.**
- It begins with a gentle melody, played *piano*, expressed by the many naturals instead of sharps.
- The melody moves in the quiet rhythm of a *siciliano*: an Italian dance in compound metre with a swaying rhythm and a pastoral theme.
- It contains many expressive wide leaps, emphasising chromatic semitone movement and the melancholy-sounding 'Neapolitan sixth' chord.
- **Ternary form: A (A1, A2, A3) B A (A1, A2, A2 Coda).**
- **Key: f sharp minor**
- Metre: 6/8
- Instrumentation is the same as the first movement

A

- **Three themes: 2A, 2B, 2C**
  2A: Bars 1–4

- Piano
- Slow tempo
- Dotted rhythms
- Large interval jumps
- Chromatic movement
- Syncopated rhythm
- Ends with perfect cadence.

2B: Bars 12–20

- Canon between violins, clarinet and bassoon
- Step movement
- Syncopated rhythm
- Arpeggio accompaniment.

2C: Bars 20–34

- Piano plays it twice
- Ornamented
- Chromatic
- Descending scales
- Developed and a modulation to the relative major, A major.

B

- A major
- Piano and clarinet
- Broken-chord accompaniment in triplets
- Right-hand demi-semiquaver runs.

A

- Main themes are developed but the orchestration remains quite similar to the opening section.
- New textures are added in the **Coda**, the sighing melody from the canon is heard against a repeated piano dominant notes before the movement gradually fades away.

Allegro assai, third movement

Third movement: themes

Exposition	Development Section	Recapitulation	Coda
SIa Theme A	Episodes	Theme B	SIa 'A' SIIb
SIb	Theme E	SIIa 'C'	'D' Finale
Theme B SIIa Theme C SIIb Theme D SIa (codetta or transition)	Theme F	SIIb 'D'	based on SIb
Key: A–em–E	f#m—D—A	A—am—A	A—D—A

SIa is Theme A, the recurring main theme of the rondo. It is also the First subject (SI) 'a' theme – SIa.

SIb is a motif in the first subject group. It is not a recurring theme in the rondo but is used at the very end of the concerto.

Theme B could also be called **SIc**, as it is part of the first subject grouping. In sonata form proper, it would be a bridge theme before the second subject melodies.

Form

- An extended **sonata-rondo**: a recurrent first theme alternates with a number of episodes (rondo), but unusually one of those episodes also returns, as a second theme would do in a sonata recapitulation.

- The fusion of these two forms results in a structure that allows the main melodies to be heard over and over again, while the alternations and developments of those melodies afford Mozart infinite diversity in compositional development.

- **Metre**: cut common time

- **Key**: A major

- Mozart offers an overabundance of themes with some drama in the middle before the high spirits of the opening return to carry the concerto to its finish.

Exposition

Theme A

Subject Ia

- Piano

- Fast and virtuosic movement

- Alberti bass accompaniment

- Orchestra takes over them

Subject Ib

- Strings against woodwind.

Theme B

- Solo piano

- Slow, graceful melody

- Grace notes

- Staccato

- Imperfect cadence at end.

Theme C

- E minor
- Introduced by flute and bassoon accompanied by strings
- Continues with the piano's never-ending arpeggios and scales and with varying styles of accompaniment.

Theme D

- E major
- Repeated notes
- Pizzicato strings
- Pedal note on horn.

Development

- Two new contrasting episodes
- Theme E and theme F
- F# minor scale passage (**Theme E**)
- D major lyrical melody
- Mozart's development of the musical material is perfect. The fragments of themes are always audible, the texture, while interesting, is not over-complicated, while the modulations are flawless.

Recapitulation

- An ornamented version of Theme B
- Piano repeated by woodwind
- A minor
- Theme C
- A major
- Woodwind repeated on piano
- The music strides forward with richer textures and more counterpoint before the coda is introduced. These tutti passages are as bright and lively as Mozart ever composed.

Coda

- Dialogue between violin, flute and horn.

Berlioz: Symphonie Fantastique

OVERVIEW

- Berlioz subtitled this work 'Episode in the Life of an Artist'.

- The symphony follows a **five-movement structure** (like Beethoven's Sixth Symphony, the 'Pastoral').

- Just like Beethoven, Berlioz provides the movements with headings and lays out a **story** that the symphony will follow.

- But, going even further than Beethoven in instrumentation, atmosphere and structure, Berlioz laid out the concept of what is now called **programme music**.

- The five movements express Berlioz's dreams regarding his obsession with his first wife Harriet Smithson (an Anglo-Irish actress).

- Berlioz distributed the programme notes to the audience before the performance of the symphony. This provided some musical understanding to the listener. The images Berlioz is portraying in each movement can help you remember the musical analysis when you listen to the music.

- Berlioz is surprisingly **modern**; he uses a very large orchestra. Although it belongs to an early Romantic genre, Berlioz's music was stylistically original.

- Colourful orchestration and tone colour (timbre) is used throughout, including bells, cor anglais, two harps, multi-divisi strings, timpani and a large brass section. This was considered a huge orchestra in 1830.

- Berlioz's loved one is represented by an **idée fixe** (a principle later adopted by Wagner – the leitmotif). All of the movements are unified by a **recurring theme**, the idée fixe. The idée fixe is musically varied in each movement.

- Berlioz broke with tradition. His second movement (Valse: *Un Bal*) takes the place of the traditional scherzo.

INSTRUMENTS USED IN *UN BAL*

- 2 flutes/piccolo, oboe, 2 clarinets
- 4 horns
- Strings (violins I, violins II, violas, cellos and double basses) and 2 harps. (Originally, Berlioz had asked for four harps, two doubling the first harp part and two doubling the second harp part.)

INSTRUMENTS USED IN *MARCHE AU SUPPLICE*

- 2 flutes/piccolo, oboe , 2 clarinets, 4 bassoons
- 4 horns, 2 trumpets, 2 cornets, 3 trombones, 2 ophicleides (tuba-like instrument)
- 4 timpani, cymbals, bass drum, side drum
- Strings (violins I [divided], violins II [divided], violas [divided], cellos and double basses) and 2 harps.

SAMPLE QUESTIONS ON *UN BAL*

Question: From which movement does this excerpt come?

Answer: *Un Bal* **or second movement.**

- Don't write '*Un Bal*' **and** 'first movement'. If you give an incorrect movement number but the correct movement name, an examiner may cancel your marks altogether.

Question: Where in *Un Bal* is this excerpt found?

- You could write 'start', 'middle' or 'end' and you may gain some marks, but it's best to be more specific.
- Pin down your answer to a description such as 'introduction', 'A section', 'Coda', etc.
- Learn the **form** of each movement of each of your Set Works. Be able to reference them from memory.

Question: What is the tonality/key of this excerpt/movement?

- **Tonality** refers to major, minor, modal, tonal, atonal, etc.
- **Key** means you have to specify the actual key signature. For example: 'The key and tonality of this movement is **A major**.'
- Writing the answer 'A' will gain full marks, since 'A' is taken to mean 'A major'.
- The first **idée fixe** is in F major.
- Remember: the introduction has major, minor and diminished chords and the **tonality** isn't settled until well into the introduction.

Question: What instrumental techniques are heard in this excerpt?

- Pizzicato and tremolo (strings) are the only real 'instrumental techniques' found in *Un Bal*.

- Arco (bowing) is the normal playing style for string instruments so you are unlikely to be awarded marks for stating this.

Question: Name the cadence heard at bar X.

- When identifying cadences, use the **names** of the cadences (i.e. perfect, imperfect, plagal or interrupted), not the chord numbers (unless specifically asked to do so).

Second movement: *Un Bal*

- **Programme:** This movement begins with a sense of anticipation. The composer enters the ballroom filled with waltzing dancers and sees his beloved through the crowd (**idée fixe**).
- **Key:** A major
- **Metre:** 3/8
- **Form:** Ternary (Intro, A, B, A1, Coda).

Introduction

- Tremolo strings, ascending arpeggi in major, minor and diminished chords
- Descending scales form a perfect cadence in the tonic.
- 'Um-pah-pah' waltz-type accompaniment in the lower strings.

A Main Theme 1

- A 16-bar melody in violin I uses **rubato**.

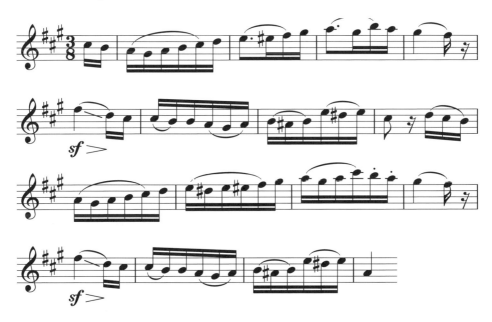

- Simple tonic arpeggi on harp and lower strings introduce Theme 2, again in violin I. This theme is a **descending scale**.

- The answering phrase (also of five bars in length) uses semiquaver triplets in an ornamental turn-like fashion and employs **chromatics**.

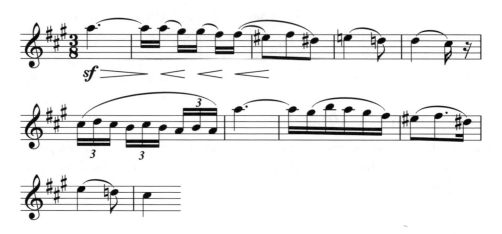

- Flute and clarinets provide the **bridge**, a major scale in 3rds, to **Theme 3**.

- The opening phrase to this melody is a descending sequence of repeated notes, while the texture of the answering phrase is polyphonic.

- A **canon** (at a crotchet) is used in contrary motion (violin I and cello).

- Theme 1 is repeated with a varied accompaniment of strings, harp and wind chords on each quaver beat respectively.

B The Idée Fixe

- The **idée fixe** is interwoven into this middle episode in the distant key of **F major**, despite the ongoing waltz rhythm, appearing in the flute and oboe (then flute and clarinet).

- The accompaniment is extremely soft **tremolo** violin and viola murmurs above **staccato arpeggi** in cello and bass.

- The accompaniment becomes more substantial and **contrapuntal** as the violins overlap with a semiquaver descant.

A1 The Recapitulation

- A1 The **recapitulation** uses the three main themes again in the tonic (A major) with an elongated and developed Theme 1 being repeated.

- The orchestration is much fuller and the texture more **polyphonic** in Theme 1 and Theme 3 with ornamented violin I lines and more use of block harmony in the wind in Theme 2.

- The **idée fixe** appears in the **coda**; a solo clarinet over flute and **horn pedal notes** (homophonic texture).

- A faster **tutti** rendition of Theme 1 leads to the lively cadential ending.

Fourth movement: *Marche au Supplice*

- **Programme:** The composer dreams that he has murdered his beloved and has been condemned to die 'at the scaffold'.

- **Key:** G minor. (March section in B flat major – piece ends in G major.)

- **Metre:** Cut common time

- **Form:** Introduction, Main Section 1 (Descending theme), Main Section 2 (March theme), Transition–Development, Coda.

Introduction

- Long crescendo, opening timpani ostinato and syncopated bassoon and horn figure successfully create the dark mood and tension.

Main Section 1 (Descending theme)

- The **Descending theme** (two octaves) is a scale of **g melodic minor**.

- It is first heard in the cellos and basses and ends in an imperfect cadence.
- The **second rendition** of this theme adds violas with the four bassoons playing a syncopated countermelody.

- The **third time** (and **fourth time**) the violins play the descending theme in E flat two octaves higher in pitch. A walking bass accompaniment is heard in the lower strings (this sounds like a new countermelody).

- The **fifth rendition** uses the descending theme in inversion and contrary motion in the strings accompanied by the bassoon playing a staccato walking bass.

Main Section 2 (March theme)

- Timpani B flats and a sweep of a B flat scale on strings introduce the March theme. A syncopated, dotted fanfare-like melody played by wind and brass.

- This theme is repeated. Berlioz uses **antiphonal blocks of sound** (brass answered by woodwind) and fragments the descending theme until the March theme is reiterated in B flat, this time with elaborate string accompaniments.
- Fuller textured sequential developments of the descending theme against a sextuplet accompaniment in woodwind and rising ornamented crotchets in the strings follow.
- A *ff tutti* statement of the descending theme is heard in the tonic key.

Coda

- Dotted string fragments are juxtaposed against wind repeated chords and the tension increases.
- Suddenly, the sparsely contrasted **idée fixe appears in the clarinet** (monophonic texture) just before the execution by guillotine, the loud cadential conclusion ending in G major (*tierce de picardie*).

BERLIOZ USES A MIXTURE OF ITALIAN AND FRENCH TEMPO MARKINGS:

- **Iº tempo:** Original tempo.
- **Iº tempo con fuoco:** Original tempo with fire.
- **Allegretto non troppo:** Not too fast.
- **Animez:** Animated (faster).
- **q = 60:** Metronome mark, 60 crotchets per minute (one per second).
- **Rall ... a tempo:** Slowing ... back to speed.
- **Rall. poco:** A little slower.
- **Sans retenir:** Without holding back.
- **Serrez:** Densely.
- **Un peu retenu:** A little held back.
- **Valse:** Allegro non troppo (not too fast, waltz speed).

INSTRUMENTAL TECHNIQUES AND EXPRESSION MARKINGS

- **A 4 soli**: All four bassoons play one line.
- **Arco**: With the bow.
- **Avec les cylinders, tous les son ouvert**: Open bell (horns).
- **Baguettes d'éponge**: Use of soft sticks (timpani).
- **Canto**: Singing.
- **Dim.**: Diminuendo, dying away.
- **Div. (diviso)**: Divided (instrumental parts).
- **Dolce e tenero**: Sweetly and held.
- **Espressivo**: Expressively.
- **Étouffez le son avec la main**: Dampen the sound with your hand.
- **Faites les sons bouchés avec le main sans employer les cylinders**: Put hand in the bell (horns).
- **Flauto 2 muta in flauto piccolo**: Second flute to piccolo.
- **[mf]**: Editorial markings appear in square brackets.
- **Molto**: Much.
- **Observez bien ici, la difference entre le fort et le demi-fort**: Be careful of the difference between *ff* and *mf*.
- **Pizz.**: Plucking.
- **Poco**: Little.
- **Presque rien**: Almost nothing.
- **Rinf**: Rinforzando (play very loudly and come away suddenly).
- **Sempre**: Always.
- **Soli**: Plural of solo.
- **Unis.**: Unison.
- **8**: Play one octave higher than written.

Raymond Deane: *Seachanges (with Danse Macabre)*

You should be able to:

- describe the sections, form and structure of the piece
- examine all compositional devices used: harmonic, melodic, rhythmic and metric
- identify the instruments used in each section
- explain the workings of the tone row (main melody)
- define the modern instrumental techniques used by each instrument
- describe the themes and sentiment behind the work.

OVERVIEW

- This chamber work deals irreverently with the theme of **death**.
- The grey, misty Irish Atlantic is set against the clear, bright Mexican Pacific.
- The piece was influenced by **Mexican iconography**, which is morbid, grotesque and gaudily melodramatic.
- In composing the piece, Deane had in mind a section from Shakespeare's *The Tempest*: 'Full fathom five thy father lies'.
- American composer Conlon Nancarrow was a resident of Mexico. The **canon** between violin and marimba in *Seachanges* is dedicated to him.

Instruments used in *Seachanges*

- Piccolo
- Crotales (bells)
- Alto flute
- Maracas

- Piano
- Gong
- Violin
- Marimba

- Cello
- Güiro
- Cymbals
- Rainstick.

The Mexican or exotic instruments (the güiro, maracas, guitar [strumming like a guitar on the cello and violin] and marimba) contrast sharply with the European instruments. The piccolo and alto flute have high pitched timbres that may represent the sounds of seabirds; and the piano is used melodically to represent the misty Irish coastline on a dull morning.

No Italian tempo markings are used in *Seachanges* and there are only two strict metronome markings, which alternate throughout the piece:

$$\text{♩} = 80 \quad \text{and} \quad \text{♩} = 120$$

Form	Section Name	Features	Bars
A	Introduction	Main melody	1–20
A1	Section 1	Main melody and inversion	21–45
B	Section 2	Totentanz	46–68
	Link	Development of Totentanz	69–73
A2	Section 3	Main melody and inversion	74–91
C	Section 4	Dies Irae	92–127
A3	Section 5	Main melody	128–140
B1 and C1	Section 6	Totentanz and Dies Irae	141–174

Instrumental techniques

- **Arco:** Play with the bow.
- **Col legno bat.:** Play with the wood of the bow.
- **Con ped.:** With pedal.
- **Fz.:** Flute, flutter tonguing.
- **Gliss.:** Glissando (slide).
- **Loco:** Place, cancelling an 8ba marking etc.
- **L.v.:** Let vibrate.

- **Modo ord.**: Play normally.
- **Molto vib.**: Much vibrato.
- **Non troppo cresc.**: Not too much louder.
- **Pizz +**: Left-hand pizzicato.
- **Sec. (secco)**: Dry (no pedal).
- **Sempre**: Always.
- **Sfffz**: Sforzandissimo, (suddenly very, very loud).
- **Strum**: Strum cello like a guitar.
- **Sul pont.**: Play near the bridge.
- **Sul tasto**: Bow over the fingerboard.
- **Tr.**: Trill.
- **Tremolo**: Trembling effects.
- **U.C.**: Una corda (left 'soft' pedal on piano).
- **8ba**: Play an octave lower than written.
- **8va**: Play one octave higher than written.
- **15ma**: Play 2 octaves higher than written – harmonics.

Compositional techniques include:

- subtraction principle
- augmentation
- inversion
- canon
- diminution
- addition.

Contrasts in dynamics and timbres

- An important feature of this work is the huge **dynamic range** and varied and sudden dynamic contrasts.
- The use of **resonant** instruments (cymbals, crotales, gong) are also well contrasted against the *sec.* (dry) sounds; *pizz+*, maracas and syncopated piano chords.
- The piano acts as a link between the dynamic and resonant timbre qualities of all the other instruments.

A Introduction

- Main motif: three-note cell (GAC)

- Changing time signatures
- Descending chords on piano.

A1 Main melody and inversion

- Main melody on violin; inversion on cello

- Harmonics on violin
- Subtraction principle
- Marimba, piccolo, piano – inversion.

B Totentanz

- Rhythmic section
- Maracas followed by strings and güiro

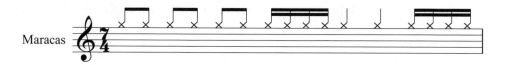

- Percussion sounds on violin and cello
- Main melody is heard on piano *fff*.

A2 Main melody and inversion

- Main melody on violin, in minims

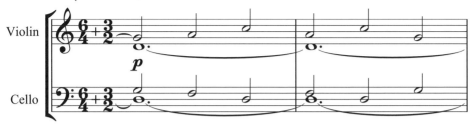

- Inversion on cello, in minims
- Subtraction principle
- Countermelody on flute – improvisatory in style
- Rainstick is introduced.

C Dies Irae

- Canon on marimba and violin
- 7/8 throughout
- Güiro playing in the background
- Chromaticism used throughout this section
- Subtraction principle
- Piano clusters.

A3 Main melody

- Augmentation also used as a compositional device
- Main melody for flute and piano
- Very low and very slow
- 6/4, 3/2
- Totentanz rhythm in triplets on the marimba
- **Addition principle** also used in A3 section. The piano accompaniment starts with just one chord and builds to eight chords, while the alto flute theme is being reduced, one note at a time.
- Change of tempo at the end.

B1 and C1 Totentanz and Dies Irae

- Totentanz rhythm on C major chord in the string parts
- Canon idea
- Free flute style
- Piano clusters
- As the music progresses it gets more rhythmic rather than melodic, more percussive
- Totentantz is played on violin and cello
- All end with the maracas to end of piece.

HARMONIC ANALYSIS

- Overall, the piece has an **atonal** tonality. There is no key centre, but the three-note row (or four-note row including D) is the closest sounding 'tonal' centre in the piece.
- The note G is central to the Introduction and Section 1.
- The note D is the pedal note (in the cello) in Section 3.
- The note E flat is the central note in Section 5.
- C major chords (on strings, double stopping) are important in the final section, Section 6. Here we see bi-tonality, where other instruments play against the C major chords in dissonance.
- The piece ends on the next most important note, A.

FEATURES

- The open strings can be used in double, triple or quadruple stopping while maintaining the row. Playing on an 'open' string cannot produce vibrato. This effect is eerie and sounds almost medieval.
- Complex rhythmic patterns and rhythmic counterpoint are abundant in this work.
- Frequently changing time signatures also give the work a vacillating pulse. Deane uses the device of rhythmic displacement and cross rhythms to also help syncopate the pulse.

The Beatles: *Sgt. Pepper's Lonely Hearts Club Band*

Sgt. Pepper's Lonely Hearts Club Band was released in 1967 and held the number-one position for twenty-seven weeks in the UK, and nineteen weeks in the US. The main people involved in the recording were:

- Paul McCartney: vocals and bass guitar
- John Lennon: vocals and guitar
- George Harrison: lead guitar and vocals
- Ringo Starr: drums
- George Martin: production and arrangement.

You should be able to identify:

- unusual chord progressions
- static melody
- counterpoint in the horn interlude
- drum kit/guitar backbeat patterns
- John Lennon's distinctive voice in the chorus
- descending chromatic bass guitar line.

Expression markings

- 𝄋 and Dal Segno al Coda: Back to the sign and then to the Coda.

- 𝄐 : Pause.
- Tacet: Silence.

'Sgt. Pepper's Lonely Hearts Club Band'

- Composer: Paul McCartney.
- Key: G major.
- Metre: 4/4.

- Tempo: Moderately slow, with strong beat.
- Form: Intro (instrumental)/Verse/Bridge (instrumental)/Refrain (chorus)/Bridge (vocal)/Verse/Coda (segue or link).
- Recorded on 1 and 2 February, 3 and 6 March 1967 in Abbey Road.
- Additional instruments: four French horns (players from the London Philharmonic Orchestra).
- Mood: The mood is one of vibrancy. The loud rock sounds and recording studio effects of audience and orchestra tuning up give an impression of an open-air concert.
- Style and form: Hard syncopation and bluesy bent notes. Typically 1960s rock/pop style, but with fusion of classical elements.
- The song is just two minutes in length and about ten seconds of that is the opening mix of crowd and tuning noises.
- In the opening seconds of the track, we hear a rather passive **audience** chatting indistinctly amongst themselves. In the background, a **string section** is **tuning up**. Once the music starts, the audience becomes more active. We hear applause and laughter. The final verse brings more applause and screaming, perhaps a nod to 'Beatlemania'.
- Vocal arrangement: Paul McCartney sings solo in rock style for the verses; a chorus is provided by the other band members for the refrain and second bridge.
- Instrumentation: Electric lead guitar, four French horns, rhythm guitar, lead vocal, bass guitar and vocal harmony in chorus.
- Homophonic and polyphonic textures.
- Key change for interlude.
- Repetition.

Introduction: Bars 1–4

- The track fades in with more than ten seconds of concert hall audience ambience and orchestral tuning.
- Lead guitar takes over the melody in a quasi-blues/rock style.
- The opening chord is not chord I, it is V7 of V. This is a very typical Beatles chord: the dominant of the dominant – secondary dominant.
- The chord sequence is: G/A7/C7/G.

Verse 1

- The verse is a standard eight bars long.
- Homophonic texture.
- Repeated notes.

- Syncopation.
- Semi-quaver vocal line.
- The melodic shape is quite static, which gives a rhetorical, declamatory feel to the singing.
- The vocal part of the last four bars of the verse places repeated emphasis on the flattened blues third, turning the C chord into a C7, and creating a major–minor cross-relation in the last against the tonic chords.

Bridge

- The instrumental bridge is five bars long.
- Four French horns.
- Contrapuntal style.
- Much reverb is used.
- The two bridges are differentiated by their different arrangements and melodic content.
- Instrumental bridge opens with a V7 (dominant seventh) chord on C. This makes the first half of the music sound like a modulation to the key of F major (a distance key from the tonic, G major).

Refrain

- This is the song's main chorus and it is the longest of the sections. It reiterates many times the words of the title.
- Vocal line changes from semi-quaver movement to quaver movement.
- There are two- and three-part vocal harmonies.
- Harmonic dissonances are abundant: the major/minor switch on the I chord (with the minor one presented in first inversion); the appoggiatura on the C chord; the bluesy minor third in the tune clashing with the D chord and the implied V9 chord.

Coda

- Chords vamped over a stepwise descending bass line.
- Direct segue into the next track ('With a Little Help from my Friends') is an interesting experiment on this album.

'She's Leaving Home'

- Composers: John Lennon and Paul McCartney.
- Instruments: String nonet – four violins, two violas, two cellos, a double bass and a harp.
- It is the first song on the album not to include guitars and drums.

- Key: E major in the stereo recording (F major in the mono recording) and E flat major in the piano score.
- Metre: 3/4.
- Tempo: Moderately.
- Form: Intro/Verse 1/Refrain/Verse 2/Refrain/Verse 3/Refrain/Coda.
- Recorded on 17 and 20 March 1967 in Abbey.
- Mood: Melancholy.
- Style: Fusion of pop and classical.
- An intentionally **over-lush impression** is created with the wide, sweeping range of the melody.
- Teeming usage of **seventh** and **ninth chords**.
- **Flattened seventh** notes and **minor v (dominant)**. There is a Mixolydian modal feeling.
- The backing vocals for the refrains feature an unusual kind of **antiphonal counterpoint**.
- The **string parts** fill the spaces between verse phrases and anticipate some of the melodic play of the refrain.
- **No modulations** in this piece.
- Homophonic and polyphonic textures.
- **Word-painting**.
- **Syncopated rhythms** in strings.
- **Counterpoint** in instruments and voices in refrain.
- Melodic line in **cellos**.
- Repeated chords.
- Unusual phrasing.
- Unusual chords.

Introduction

- The introduction consists of four bars of harp playing an elaborate arpeggio in the tonic chord.

Verse

- The homophonic verse is in the phrase pattern **ABAB**. The harmonic rhythm continually slows down.
- There is a rising and falling **melodic minor countermelody** in the cellos.

- Syncopated rhythms and **contrary motion patterns** in the strings break the constant simple 3/4 accompaniments.
- The **third verse** is much shorter and has an **AB** pattern.

Refrain (Chorus)

- Polyphonic: Counterpoint in the two vocal parts (nearly antiphonal singing). Both voices are **double tracked** to produce a **chorus effect**.
- Unusual lengths of phrases; interrupted by three accented II9 chords.
- V7 of V (secondary dominant) is allowed to **resolve directly to I** (tonic) at the start of the next verse, without the benefit of the V (dominant) chord intervening.

Coda

- The final refrain includes the echoing of the harp arpeggio of the introduction.
- The V-of-V to IV is a much favoured progression of the Beatles, though the **plagal** IV–I final cadence echoes the faintly religious sentimentality.

'When I'm Sixty-Four'

- Composers: John Lennon and Paul McCartney.
- Instruments: Two clarinets, bass guitar, rhythm guitar, bass guitar, piano, drum and chimes.
- Key: C major (piano score), D flat major (original recording).
- Metre: Cut common time (2/2) written as (4/4) in some scores.
- Tempo: Steady 2 beat.
- Form: Intro/Verse/Bridge/Verse/Bridge/Verse/Coda.
- Recorded on 6, 8, 20 and 21 December 1966 in Abbey Road.
- Stylised **nostalgic/vaudeville** (music hall) song.
- In the context of *Sgt Pepper's* running order, it provides a much-needed contrast to the preceding track.
- The song is **mastered in the key of D flat**, though it was **recorded in the key of C** in order to sound higher on playback and give Paul McCartney's lead vocal a younger, more earnest quality.
- There is no doubling up of any sections, and the intro and coda use the same material.
- There is no specific refrain section, though the last phrase of the verse is **refrain-like**.
- Syncopation.
- Two-part vocal line.
- Chromatic melody.

- The tune is built primarily out of **triadic riffs** and **chromatic runs**.
- The harmony is very straightforward, but because of the chromaticisms of the melody there are many added note chords: e.g. V13, and harmonising of the chromatic bass line motion.

Introduction

- The band vamps in true vaudeville style.
- Dotted rhythm with heavy accents in **cut common metre**.
- Two clarinets in imitation.

Verse

- Chromatically rising bass lines of the second and fourth phrases.
- Each of the phrases commences with the same chord with which the previous phrase ended.
- Syncopated rhythm.
- Texture is homophonic.
- Phrases plan: ABA1C.

Bridge

- The bridge is an unusual seventeen bars long; sixteen plus one.
- The harmony in this section suggests a modal modulation to the key of the relative minor, and then back to the tonic key.
- Alberti bass in the piano accompaniment.
- Jazz style on the clarinet.
- Polyphonic texture.
- Chimes come in at the end of the bridge section.

HIGHER LEVEL QUESTION 3, 2009

HL

An excerpt from Symphonie Fantastique by Berlioz will be played THREE times. There is a twenty second gap between each playing of the music in this question. There is no printed music for this question.
Answer the following questions:

(i) Name the movement from which this excerpt is taken.

_____

It is taken from the:
❐ beginning   ❐ middle   ❐ end

(ii) This excerpt features a descending:
❐ major scale   ❐ major arpeggio   ❐ minor scale   ❐ minor arpeggio
It is played by:

_____

(iii) The texture of the excerpt is mostly:
❐ monophonic   ❐ homophonic   ❐ polyphonic

Explain your answer with reference to the music heard in this excerpt.

_____

_____

_____

(iv) Describe the tempo at the end of the excerpt.

_____

_____

(v) The last three melody notes are

(10 marks)

HIGHER LEVEL QUESTION 4, 2009

An excerpt from Seachanges (with Danse Macabre) *by Deane will be played* THREE *times. There is a twenty second gap between each playing of the music in this question. There is no printed music for this question.*

Answer the following questions:

(i) Which theme is heard in this excerpt?

_____

(ii) In the table below, write down the order (1–3) in which the instruments listed are heard at the start of the excerpt.

Instrument	Order
Piano	
Violin	
Maracas	

(iii) The instrumental technique illustrated below is heard in this excerpt. Describe this technique and identify the instrument(s) with which it is associated.

Technique _____

Instrument(s) _____

(iv) Describe one feature of the music played by the piano in this excerpt.

_____

_____

_____

(v) How does Deane portray the spirit of the Danse Macabre in this excerpt?

_____

_____

_____

(10 marks)

5 Irish Traditional Music

aims
- To learn about the characteristics of Irish traditional music, past and present.

Question 5 on the Listening Paper

This question is divided as follows:

Higher Level:
- Listening – 15 marks
- Essay – 10 marks.

Ordinary Level:
- Listening – 25 marks.

Listening

- There are usually three excerpts on which the questions are based.
- The excerpts often include: a dance form, a song and a modern/fusion piece.
- You must be able to distinguish between the melody, rhythmic and accompaniment instruments.
- Identification of dance tune types and vocal styles is essential.
- You must know the different timbres of the instruments.
- A knowledge of Irish traditional musical characteristics (traditional and non-traditional) should be evident.

- Be familiar with fusions of Irish music and other styles.
- Aim to display your knowledge of past and ongoing developments and styles in Irish traditional music.

TRADITIONAL INSTRUMENTS	NON-TRADITIONAL INSTRUMENTS
• accordion/melodeon	• banjo
• bodhrán	• bouzouki
• concertina	• drum kit
• fiddle	• ethnic instruments
• flute	• guitar
• harp	• harpsichord
• spoons	• keyboard
• tin whistle	• mandolin
• uilleann pipes.	• orchestral instruments
	• synthesiser.

DANCE/TUNE TYPES

- single jig/double jig
- slip jig
- reel
- hornpipe
- slide
- polka
- slow air.

IRISH SONGS

- working songs
- laments/caoineadh/goltraí
- love songs/geantraí
- humorous songs
- drinking songs
- aisling
- macaronic songs (bilingual).

TRADITIONAL FEATURES

- solo performance
- group performance in unison
- ornamentation
- tune type
- traditional instruments used.

NON-TRADITIONAL FEATURES

- non-traditional instruments used
- harmony
- syncopation
- dynamics
- fusion of styles.

STYLES OF MUSIC THAT HAVE OCCURRED IN QUESTION 5:

- traditional
- folk
- ballad
- céilí band
- Irish/classical.

- Irish/ethnic
- Irish/jazz
- Irish/pop/modern/techno
- Irish/rock.

If you are asked about characteristics of Irish traditional music, you must decide whether the listening excerpt is: **traditional** (historical/music from the past); twentieth-century or **present-day** Irish traditional music; or **fusion**.

For the purposes of Leaving Certificate Music, 'traditional' usually refers to a solo, unaccompanied form; 'present-day' involves accompaniment/harmony/group performance (non-traditional); and ornamentation and dance forms are usual to both.

Essay

There is usually a choice of **four essay-style questions**. Be familiar with essay topics from past papers. These include:

- sean nós singing
- collectors
- fusion/significant developments in Irish traditional music in the twentieth century
- Irish dance music (tune types)
- ornamentation
- the harping tradition
- the influence of Irish traditional music on the folk music of North America and other countries
- composers/group performers/solo performers
- instruments.

A very short history of Irish traditional music

Medieval to early seventeenth century

Irish society consisted of the aristocracy, the commoners and the professional learned class, which included the *file* (poet) and the *reacaire* (harpist). European styles of Renaissance and early Baroque music failed to influence the Irish tradition.

Seventeenth and eighteenth centuries: two traditions

Fiddlers, pipers and ballad singers thrived in this era and their cultural musical tradition was the mainstay of the Irish people. The musical traditions of the 'Big Houses' and the middle class inside the Pale were becoming more influenced by Italian classical music, including operas and oratorios. The Belfast Harp Festival of 1792 was organised to 'revive and perpetuate the ancient music and poetry of Ireland'.

Nineteenth century: emigration and the deterioration of Irish music culture

The Great Famine and the mass emigration that followed it led to the decline of musicians, dance masters and the use of the Irish language. Much traditional folklore was lost within Ireland, but traditional Irish music became part of the fabric of life abroad, particularly in countries such as the US and Australia. During this time, many traditional tunes and songs were anglicised and they became part of the culture of the middle and upper classes.

Twentieth-century revival of Irish traditional music

With national independence and with slow but steady economic development, a new breed of traditional musician was born: one who could revive old folklore and interpret it for a twentieth-century world. Céilí bands were formed; radio and television programmes and recordings promoted Irish traditional music like never before; and Seán Ó Riada and Comhaltas Ceoltóirí Éireann (CCÉ) initiated structures that helped to develop a positive attitude towards Irish traditional music, which has increased over the last few decades.

Sean nós singing

This 'old style' of traditional singing is unique to Ireland. It is a highly skilled solo art form that dates back many centuries. Themes and stories in the songs are usually about human life: birth, love, suffering, emigration and death. Sean nós singing remains popular in areas where the Irish language has survived: Cork, Donegal, Galway, Kerry, Mayo, Meath and Waterford.

Sean nós has distinctive features:

- It involves solo singing.
- Usually there are no dynamics, expression or vibrato.
- The most important things are the words and the story being told, so the rhythm of the song is dictated by speech and syllable patterns.
- There are both Irish- and English-language songs in existence; some even use a mixture of both languages (macaronic).
- Ornamentation is generally used. Singers can embellish their performance by varying the melody and rhythm.
- There is not much repetition in songs.
- Modal scales are often used.
- A nasal tone quality is sometimes used (nasalisation).
- There is no strict tempo – free rhythm and rubato tempo.
- The singing is melismatic – more than one note is sung on each speech syllable.
- Glottal stops and dramatic pauses are used.
- Sliding or glissando is a common feature.

Each sean nós singer has a unique style. You should listen to lots of examples of sean nós singing from artists such as Mairéad Ní Mhaonaigh, Máire Begley, Tríona Ní Dhomhnaill, Muireann Nic Amhlaoibh, Iarla Ó Lionáird, Lillis Ó Laoire.

Make specific reference to the listening excerpts when answering exam questions. If there is no glottal stopping in an excerpt, you won't get marks for writing 'glottal stop' as a feature of the excerpt!

As part of your exam preparation, look up the following songs on YouTube:

- 'Jimmy Mo Mhíle Stór' (Dolores Keane, Cara Dillon, etc.)
- 'Aisling Gheal' (accompanied and unaccompanied versions by Iarla Ó Lionáird)
- 'An Mhaighdean Mhara' (Mairéad Ní Mhaonaigh).

There are three main regions associated with sean nós singing: Munster, Connemara and Donegal.

- **Donegal** sean nós has a smaller range of songs and uses little ornamentation.
- **Connemara** sean nós is melismatic and it has a nasal tone quality that uses lots of ornamentation.
- **Munster** sean nós is more like classical singing. There is a wide range of songs and some ornamentation is used.

The English language song tradition

The Irish song tradition is diverse and rich and enjoys a prominent place among the inter-related song traditions of Scotland, England and North America. Many traditional Irish songs are not sean nós-style songs. There have been many hundreds of folk songs and ballads passed down from generation to generation over the past two centuries.

Dance tunes are sometimes also 'lilted', i.e. sung with nonsense syllables. Many composed folk songs and ballads of the 1960s and 1970s have also been incorporated into this tradition. A huge variety of modern styles can be said to come under the heading of 'traditional songs', from the rebel songs of The Dubliners to the popular ballads of Mary Black, to Liam Ó Maonlaí's imaginative vocal fusion.

Regional styles

Musical style in performance is a matter of personal interpretation. Different styles are distinguishable by the musical elements used by the musicians – tempo, dynamics, amount of ornamentation used, and also the playing or singing techniques, phrasing and articulation.

In an aural tradition, players and singers have always developed the tunes that they learned by ear. This has led to many melodically similar tunes throughout the country with different titles or texts.

Before the advent of modern media, especially radio, Irish music was a local and rural tradition (apart from the tradition that emigrated to the cities of England and America). There was no national 'Irish' style of playing or singing throughout the country. There were only distinct regional styles. These different styles still exist, for example the fiddle-playing techniques of Donegal, Galway and Sligo and the sean nós singing of the provinces of Munster, Connacht and Ulster.

Fusion

Fusion is a mixture of different musical styles and traditions. Irish traditional music has been fused with many different types of music: jazz, pop, classical, rock, modern, techno and ethnic. Many traditional groups have incorporated different styles and instruments, e.g. The Chieftains, Horslips, Thin Lizzy, Kíla and Mícheál Ó Súilleabháin.

Horslips

The band was founded in Dublin by Eamon Carr, Barry Devlin, Johnny Fean, Jim Lockhart and Charles O'Connor. They are considered to be the first 'Celtic rock' group, fusing elements of traditional, country, folk and rock styles. They use a mixture of traditional and modern instruments: fiddle, uilleann pipes, whistles, banjo, bodhrán, flutes, mandolin, concertina, electric and acoustic guitars, bass guitar, keyboards and drums. They recorded ten albums in the 1970s and had number-one singles including 'Dearg Doom' and 'King of the Fairies'.

The Chieftains

The Chieftains was formed in the late 1970s and from the beginning they pushed boundaries of Irish traditional music. They used the harpsichord instead of the piano, as they thought it sounded more traditional. Other instruments used include: fiddle, flute, harp, uilleann pipes and bodhrán. The Chieftains have collaborated with musicians, singers and groups in every genre and culture: Van Morrison ('Have I Told You Lately That I Love You'), Sting ('Fields of Gold'), The Corrs, Dolly Parton and James Galway, along with orchestras from around the world. They have also experimented with Chinese and Galician music.

Thin Lizzy

This group mixed Irish music with rock. They were led by Phil Lynott. The ballad that made them famous in Ireland, Europe and America is 'Whiskey in the Jar', which they recorded in 1973.

Mícheál Ó Súilleabháin

Mícheál Ó Súilleabháin is Head of the Irish World Academy of Music and Dance in the University of Limerick. He plays the piano and has composed several compositions that fuse traditional Irish music with jazz and classical music. Examples include *Oileán* and *Becoming*.

Kíla

Kíla use flutes, uilleann pipes, violin, bodhrán and guitars. They have incorporated rock, jazz and ethnic styles into their music, which they describe as 'New Irish Music'. Pieces include 'Oh To Kiss Katie' and 'Dusty Wine Bottle'.

Fusion has become a vibrant part of the Irish traditional music scene. Bill Whelan, who composed *Riverdance*, fuses traditional and classical music in his works. Shaun Davey has several compositions that fuse traditional and classical music, e.g. 'Ripples in the Rockpool' and 'The Brendan Voyage'. De Danann have taken popular and rock songs and put a traditional stamp on them, e.g. 'Hey Jude' and 'Bohemian Rhapsody'. Other popular groups include Lúnasa and Afro Celt Sound System.

Irish traditional dances/tune types

- Dance tunes are the most common traditional Irish music played.
- Most tunes come from the eighteenth and nineteenth centuries.
- Irish dance forms were influenced by similar European dance forms.
- Jigs, reels, hornpipes and polkas are the most common dance tunes in the traditional repertoire.
- Other forms include mazurkas, slides, highlands, barn dances and céilí dance sets.
- Rhythm and the internal 'swing' is the most important feature of traditional dance music.
- Most dance tunes are in a simple repeated form, usually A and B (eight-bar phrases) repeated. Either or both of these phrases may be repeated again. The tune can then run straight into another dance producing a longer 'set' of dance tunes.
- Set dances – created by the dancing masters of the eighteenth and nineteenth centuries – are usually set to slow jigs or hornpipe rhythms.
- Slow airs are often the instrumental rendition of the melodies or 'airs' of songs, usually sean nós songs.

	Single Jig	Double Jig	Slip Jig	Reel	Hornpipe	Polka
Time signature	6/8	6/8	9/8	2/4 or 4/4	4/4	2/4
Tempo	Fast	Moderately fast	Fast	Fast	Steady dotted rhythm	Fast
Origin	England			Scotland	England	
Example	The Dublin Jig		A Fig for a Kiss	The Cavan Reel	The Liverpool Hornpipe	The Kerry Polka

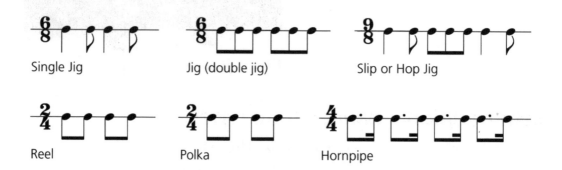

Single Jig — Jig (double jig) — Slip or Hop Jig

Reel — Polka — Hornpipe

Instruments in Irish traditional music

The core group of instruments used in Irish traditional music includes:

- Irish harp – pre-tenth century onwards
- fiddle – seventeenth century onwards
- uilleann pipes – early eighteenth century onwards
- flute – eighteenth century onwards
- accordion (button and piano) – twentieth century onwards
- concertina – 1850s onwards
- melodeon – end of nineteenth century onwards
- bodhrán
- whistles (tin whistles, low whistles)
- bones and spoons.

Non-traditional instruments used nowadays in recordings, concerts and sessions include guitar, banjo, piano, harmonica, bouzouki and many types of synthesised sounds. Identifying the melody instrument in a traditional musical extract can be difficult because sometimes many instruments play just the melodic line. Remember:

- Uilleann pipes and their drones are easy to recognise.
- You need to listen to recordings featuring accordions, fiddles, flutes, whistles, guitars, banjos and bouzoukis and analyse the **timbre** (tone colour) of each instrument.
- In a group session, like a céilí band, you may hear the piano **vamping** or a basic drum kit keeping the beat.
- Listen to recordings of some well-known traditional instrumentalists and singers and try to analyse their style. What traditional musical characteristics do they use?

Instrumentalists and singers

Harp
- Derek Bell
- Laoise Kelly.

Uilleann Pipes
- Séamus Ennis
- Paddy Moloney
- Davy Spillane
- Liam Ó Floinn
- Paddy Keenan.

Fiddle
- Michael Coleman
- James Morrison
- Frankie Gavin
- Paddy Glackin
- Mairéad Ní Mhaonaigh.

Button accordion
- Joe Cooley
- Sharon Shannon.

Flute
- Matt Molloy
- Séamus Tansey.

Tin whistle
- Seán Potts
- Mary Bergin.

Mandolin/bouzouki
- Dónal Lunny,
- Andy Irvine.

Singers
- Joe Heaney
- Tríona Ní Dhomhnaill
- Nóirín Ní Riain
- Liam Ó Maonlaí
- Paddy Tunney.

The Harp

- There are two types of Irish harp: the ancient Celtic (Gaelic) harp and the neo-Irish harp.

- *Cruit* and *cláirseach* are Irish words for the harp.

- From the fifteenth to the eighteenth century the harp was an aristocratic instrument played by professional harpers. They were employed to play in the castles and big houses. They composed music for events such as weddings, funerals and parties. They often composed pieces in honour of their patron and these pieces were known as planxties, e.g. Planxty Irwin, Planxty O'Rourke, etc.

- The harp went into decline when Ireland was under English rule.

- The oldest surviving harp is the Brian Boru Harp, which can be seen at Trinity College Dublin.

- Many harp compositions were not written down until the late sixteenth century.

- The Belfast Harp Festival began in 1792 and it aimed to revive the harp in Ireland. Edward Bunting began to collect tunes and pieces and notate them properly. He published three volumes of music known as *The Ancient Music of Ireland*.

CELTIC OR GAELIC HARP	NEO-IRISH HARP
• 22 strings made of bronze or wire	• 34/36 strings made of gut or nylon
• Plucked by fingernails	• Played with fingertips
• Resonant, rich, bell-like tone	• Softer, gentler tone
• Strings need to be dampened	• Sound does not vibrate for long
• Based on drones in F and G	• Tuned in C
• Tuned approx in B flat	• Invented by John Egan
• Made from bogwood	• Smaller version of the concert harp but without pedals
• Melody played on lower strings by the right hand	• Metal levers used to tune harp
• Turlough O'Carolan, Denis Hempson.	• Melody played in treble by right hand, left hand plays bass
	• Laoise Kelly, Janet Harbison.

Listening examples

It can be difficult to differentiate the playing styles within Irish traditional music. Below are some suggestions for listening work; you'll find most of these tunes on YouTube.

Flute

- **Matt Molloy** displays characteristics of flute-playing from the **west** of Ireland. Listen to him playing 'The Bucks of Oranmore' and you'll notice lots of ornamentation, including triplets, rolls, cuts and crans.

- **Conal Ó Gráda** has a style more characteristic of the **south** of Ireland. His playing is more aggressive, with more emphasis on the rhythm and accents on different beats.

Fiddle

- **Michael Coleman** played the fiddle in a style associated with **Sligo**. This style has been very influential style. The mood of the music is light, the tempo is very fast and the rhythm has a great lift and bounce to it. Listen to Michael playing 'Boys of the Lough'.

- The style of fiddle-playing known as **Sliabh Luachra** is distinctive. There is great life in the music, but little ornamentation is put into the tunes. Listen to Matt Cranitch and his group Sliabh Notes playing 'Three Polkas'.

- Listen to **Frankie Gavin** playing 'The Foxhunter's Reel', then listen to **Mairéad Ní Mhaonaigh** playing the same tune. Frankie Gavin is from Galway and Mairéad Ní Mhaonaigh is from Donegal. What differences in style do you hear in their playing?

HIGHER LEVEL QUESTION 5, 2008

Question 5: Irish Music
Answer A and B. Note that B contains a choice of questions.

A. You will hear THREE excerpts, each played THREE times. There is a twenty second gap between each playing of the music in this question.

Excerpt 1
  (i) Identify the type of tune heard in this excerpt.

  _____

  (ii) Identify the instrument which plays the melody.

  _____

  (iii) Identify two features of Irish traditional music which can be heard in this excerpt.

  _____

Excerpt 2
  (i) Identify the type of dance tune heard in this excerpt and its time signature.

  Dance _____ Time signature _____

  (ii) Name one instrument which plays the melody in this excerpt.

  _____

  (iii) Describe two features of this type of dance.
    1 _____
    2 _____

Excerpt 3
  (i) Identify the instrument which plays the melody.

  _____

  (ii) Describe how this piece is performed. Comment specifically on the traditional Irish features of the piece and other influences as appropriate.

  _____

  _____

B. Answer one of the following:
  (i) Identify and describe the features commonly found in sean nós singing. In your answer refer to regional styles and well-known performers.
or

(ii) Write an account of an instrumental group that you have studied in the context of traditional Irish music. In your answer refer to the style of music performed by the group and to specific pieces of music which you have heard them play.

HL

or

(iii) Discuss the contribution made by Irish folk music to the music of North America. In your answer refer to a performing style and to specific pieces of music.

or

(iv) Discuss the role of the collector in the context of Irish traditional music. In your answer refer to collectors and publications.

_____

_____

_____

_____

_____

(40 marks)

Traditional terminology

Bodhrán – simple frame drum (made with goat skin), which is beaten with a double-sided stick or the hand (fingers or knuckles).
CCÉ (Comhaltas Ceoltóirí Éireann) – a club set up in 1951 to promote Irish traditional music and dancing.
Céilí – a social occasion for traditional dancing.
Collector(s) – a person or institution (such as RTÉ, BBC) who notates (and nowadays records) the music and words of traditional music, songs and dances. This is a vital role in preserving a living aural tradition.
Fleadh Cheoil – the biggest annual festival of Irish traditional music with street sessions, classes in music, singing and dancing and concerts and competitions. Run by Comhaltas Ceoltóirí Éireann.
Hiberno-jazz – fusion of traditional Irish music with jazz characteristics.
Lilting – a singer sings a tune using nonsense words.
Sean nós – old style of traditional singing.
Session – a group or gathering of traditional musicians (and/or singers) to participate in music-making and fun.
Vamping – a type of piano accompaniment used in traditional music; usually the player plays simple chordal accompaniment patterns.

6 ▸ Aural Skills

- To understand the wider feature-based questioning in Question 6 on the Listening Paper.
- To improve listening and observational skills.

Question 6 on the Listening Paper:

- is worth **20 marks**
- examines general listening and observational skills
- can involve music from many genres: classical, jazz, rock, musical theatre, etc.
- is usually in three sections: A, B, C, each played three times
- may be three different pieces (by the same or different composers) or three sections from the one piece
- usually provides an outline score and/or lyrics.

The Leaving Certificate Music syllabus (1996) makes the following statements about Aural Skills:

2.3.4 Aural Skills

At the end of the course, all students must have:

(i) a working knowledge of musical notation …

(ii) the ability to perceive aurally and identify

- melody and rhythm within a given musical context
- vocal and instrumental timbres
- simple musical structures (binary, ternary, variation, and rondo) and the idiomatic features (melodic or rhythmic) upon which specific pieces of music are based.

In addition, Higher level students must be able:

(iii) to follow music with semiquaver movement, also music in compound time;

(iv) to perceive aurally the stylistic features that affect particular musical textures;

(v) to identify perfect, imperfect, plagal and interrupted cadences in a musical context.

In preparation for Question 6, you should:

- be familiar with Set Works
- know musical vocabulary
- listen to a variety of musical styles
- listen to CDs, watch DVDs and attend live concerts
- learn to identify instruments/voices
- listen to chords and cadences on a piano
- complete past exam papers and/or workbook questions.

Types of questions include:

- short, multiple choice and descriptive answers
- identify instruments, musical features and cadences
- circle/underline notes/words in scores/lyrics
- comment on tempo, style, instrumentation, mood, dynamics, texture, etc.
- compare/contrast two excerpts
- insert backing chords
- melodic/rhythmic dictation.

Understanding exam instructions

- Question words such as 'identify', 'name' or 'list' usually require **short** or one-word answers, e.g. 'trumpet fanfare', 'sequence', 'plagal', 'pizzicato'.

- Question words such as 'describe' or 'comment on' usually require a more elaborate answer with a more detailed analysis and **explanation**.

- 'Compare/contrast': '**compare**' means to outline the similarities within two sections/excerpts, but differences can be addressed here also. '**Contrast**' means to outline the differences only. An example of an answer to a compare/contrast question would be:

  'Excerpt one is polyphonic with strings and woodwind playing two different melodies at the same time, whereas excerpt two is homophonic with just one solo flute melody accompanied by lower strings.'

It is important to give detail in these kinds of answers. Stating 'homophonic – a melody with accompaniment' will not suffice. You must identify specific instruments/voices and explain what is actually happening in the music at that point.

USEFUL TIPS

- **Always attempt an answer.** If you write nothing, you cannot be awarded any marks; if you write something, you might pick up a mark or two!

- **Melody dictation:** Sometimes marks are awarded for 'contour' (i.e. the general shape/direction of a melody) even if all the notes are not accurate. Therefore, it's worth at least *attempting* this question. Every year, several candidates leave it completely blank and this is pointless.

- **Backing chords:** Again, never leave your answer blank here. If you really don't know the answer, you should still hazard a guess!

- Be careful with 'tick the box' questions. If you are asked to identify one instrument or feature, don't tick more than one box, as cancellation of marks could apply.

- The same applies to 'underline' or 'b' instructions. If you underline or circle several options and your answer is therefore unclear, you may be awarded no marks.

- Remember that **upper case** and **lower case** numbers are used for **major** and **minor** chords respectively.

- You will hear everything three times, so **don't panic** if you don't gather all the necessary information in the first or second hearing.

Musical features

There are **five** different categories of musical features that are usually examined here. They are:

- melodic
- harmonic
- instrumental.
- rhythmic
- compositional

Melodic refers to a feature of the tune. For example: scale, stepwise, wide leaps, 8ve leaps, sequence, repetition, high/low pitch, ascending/descending, etc.

Rhythmic refers to a feature of the rhythm. For example: dotted/bumpy, syncopated, triplets, etc.

Harmonic refers to a feature of the harmony/chords. For example: major/minor/diminished chords; sustained/block/ broken/alberti chords; monophonic/homophonic/polyphonic/contrapuntal textures.

Compositional refers to the devices used by the composer in composing the music. This includes all of the above mentioned features. In addition, you could include features such as: imitation, canon, contrary motion, inversion, diminution, augmentation, playing in octaves, modulation, etc.

Instrumental refers to how an instrument is played. For example: tremolo, pizzicato, glissando, sul ponticello, etc.

It is very important to translate Italian musical terms. Don't just leave them in Italian; examiners want to know that you actually understand the Italian word!

Be careful not to list the obvious techniques. For example, *arco* is the usual way of playing a stringed instrument, so you are unlikely to gain marks for listing this. An answer on instrumental techniques generally lists a special technique, such as *pizzicato*.

HIGHER LEVEL QUESTION 6, 2010

HL

This question is based on THREE excerpts of popular music. There is a twenty second gap between each playing of the music in this question.

Answer the questions on each excerpt.

Excerpt 1

The Introduction and first verse of 'One Day I'll Fly Away' by Will Jennings/Joe Sample will be played THREE times. The words of the verse only are printed below.

1. I make it alone
2. When love is gone
3. Still you made your mark
4. Here in my heart

(i) Insert the pitch and rhythm of the 5 missing notes at X played by the oboe in the introduction.

(ii) Describe the music played by the violins at the end of each line of the verse.

_____

_____

(iii) The form of the verse is

  ❏ AA1BA   ❏ ABB1A   ❏ ABAB1

Excerpt 2

The introduction and first verse of 'It's Not Unusual' by Les Reed/Gordon Mills will be played THREE times. The words only are printed below.

1. It's not unusual to be loved by anyone
2. It's not unusual to have fun with anyone
3. But when I see you hanging about with anyone
4. It's not unusual to see me cry, I wanna die.

(i) The melodic figure heard in the introduction is

It is played by

_____

(ii) Identify the tonality of this excerpt.

_____

(iii) Describe one rhythmic feature of the vocal line as heard in this excerpt.

_____

Excerpt 3

The first verse of 'Bridge Over Troubled Water' by Paul Simon will be played THREE times. The words are printed below.

1. When you're weary, feeling small
2. When tears are in your eyes, I will dry them all
3. I'm on your side, oh, when times get rough
4. And friends just can't be found
5. Like a bridge over troubled water, I will lay me down
6. Like a bridge over troubled water, I will lay me down

(i) The accompaniment in line 1 features
   ☐ a countermelody   ☐ arpeggios   ☐ a pedal note

(ii) In which line is the following melody heard?

Line _____

(iii) Describe the texture of the excerpt.

_____

Now listen to a later excerpt from the song (verse 3) which is not printed here. It will be played TWICE. Answer (iv) below.

(iv) Describe three ways in which verse 3 differs from verse 1.

1 _____

_____

2 _____

_____

3 _____

_____

(20 marks)

7 Composition Paper Essentials

exam focus

- The Composition Paper carries a total of **100 marks**.
- There is one **Harmony** question, worth **60 marks**.
- There is one **Melody** question, worth **40 marks**.
- You will have **1 hour 30 minutes** to complete both questions.

You need to know all major and minor key signatures, up to four sharps and four flats.

- C major
- G major (F#)
- D major (F#/C#)
- A major (F#/C#/G#)
- E major (F#/C#/G#/D#)
- F major (B♭)
- B♭ major (B♭/E♭)
- E♭ major (B♭/E♭/A♭)
- A♭ major (B♭/E♭/A♭/D♭)

- a minor
- e minor
- b minor
- f# minor
- c# minor
- d minor
- g minor
- c minor
- f minor

Choose an instrument suitable to the range of music given.

Rhythm groupings

- You need to know how to group rhythms in 3/4, 4/4 and 6/8.
- Be very careful when there is an upbeat.
- Start by revising the Irish Traditional Music rhythm groupings:

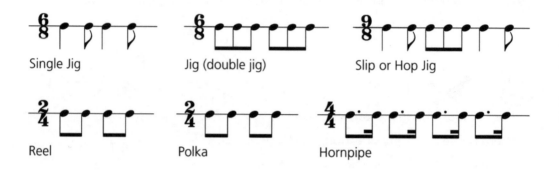

Single Jig   Jig (double jig)   Slip or Hop Jig

Reel   Polka   Hornpipe

- Ensure that you understand other rhythm groupings and dance forms, e.g. waltz, minuet, gavotte, etc.

Modulation

- Familiarise yourself with modulations from the tonic to the dominant (I to V).

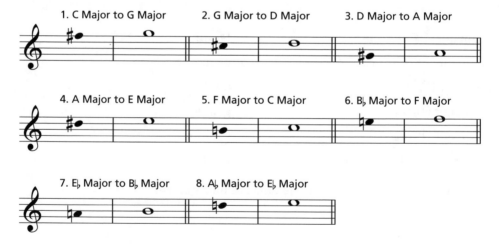

1. C Major to G Major   2. G Major to D Major   3. D Major to A Major

4. A Major to E Major   5. F Major to C Major   6. B♭ Major to F Major

7. E♭ Major to B♭ Major   8. A♭ Major to E♭ Major

Form

- A A1 B A2
- A A1 B B1

Cadences

- Perfect: V–I
- Imperfect: I–V /ii–V/IV–V/Vi–V

- Plagal: IV–I
- Interrupted: V–Vi

Sequence

- A sequence is an idea repeated up or down a note, e.g. Soh, Lah, Ti, Soh or Fa, Soh, Lah, Fa.

Developing material

Ensure that you know how to develop given material from bars 1 and 2. Try a few different things. Bar 1 is usually based on Chord I. You could invert the melody, add in passing notes, write up an octave, etc. These could also be ideas for bars 13 and 14.

Dynamics

Typical Dynamic Markings

ppp　*pp*　*p*　　　　　　*mp*　　*mf*　　　　　*f*　*ff*　*fff*
p = piano, soft　　　　*m* = mezzo, moderately　　*f* = forte, loud

crescendo　　　diminuendo

8 Melody Composition Question

aims
- To be familiar with the marking scheme for the Melody Composition question.
- To understand the best approaches to the different options on the Melody Composition question.

exam focus

- The Melody Composition question carries **40 marks**.
- There are **three questions** given and you must choose **one** to answer.
- Question 1 and Question 3 tend to be similar. The options are:
    1. **Continuation of a given text**
    2. **Setting music to a given text**
    3. **Composing to a given dance rhythm.**

MARKING SCHEME

Grade A (34–40 marks)
- Excellent melodic style and structure
- Good points of climax
- Convincing rhythm
- Development of opening ideas (good rhythm/text development).

Grade B (28–33 marks)
- Very aware of shape and structure
- Musical, with good points of climax
- Well-developed opening ideas (dance style maintained/good text setting).

Grade C (22–27 marks)
- Good sense of melodic and rhythmic interest
- Fairly well-maintained rhythmic dance style/careful text setting.

Grade D (16–21 marks)
- Careful melody and shape
- Reasonable shape and accurate rhythm (accurate word setting).

Grade E (10–15 marks)

- Little melodic interest
- Some inaccurate rhythms (inaccuracies in word setting).

Grade F (0–9 marks)

- No sense of key
- Inconsistent rhythm
- Poor structure (inconsistent word setting, poor shape).

Deductions, if omitted or deficient

- Modulation at a suitable point (4 marks)
- Phrasing (structural, articulation or both), dynamics, instrument (up to 2 each)
- Accept one correct instrument only (clef and range).

Question 1 and Question 3

- Is the **melody major or minor** (there will always be an accidental note if it is minor)?
- Is there an **upbeat**? Number your bars and put phrase marks in.
- Look at the range of music and choose a suitable **instrument**. Clarinet and violin have both got wide ranges of notes.
- Try to **hear** the melody given.
- **Write out chords.** For example:

      D major
      Chord I = D F# A
      Chord ii = E G B
      Chord iii = F# A C#
      Chord iV = G B D
      Chord V = A C# E
      Chord Vi = B D F#
      Chord Vii = C#E G

- Mark in where **modulation** and **sequence** will occur.
- Mark in where **cadences** will be.
- In your rough work, develop phrase 2: bars 1 and 2 in bars 5 and 6. Try a few different things. Bar 1 is usually based on Chord I. You could invert the melody, add in passing notes, write up an octave, etc.
- **Modulation** will go in bars 7 and 8 of phrase 2.

- Put **sequence** in bars 9 and 10.
- Put **imperfect cadence** in bars 11 and 12.
- Bars 13 and 14 need to be similar to bars 1 and 2 (look at ideas for bars 5 and 6).
- Include **dynamics**. If your composition is ascending, you should use a crescendo, e.g. *mp* to *mf*. Likewise, if composition is descending use decrescendo.
- If there is a **rest** in the opening phrase, include same bar in A1 and A2. This shows the examiner that you are following the style.
- Continue **articulation** if it is used in opening phrase.
- It is very important that you **check your composition thoroughly**. Check your modulation, sequence, dynamics, instrument, phrasing and cadences before you finish this question.

Minor composition

- Raise the 7th note.
- If the melody moves 6th–7th note make sure you **raise** both notes.
- If the melody moves 7th–6th notes, make sure you **lower** both notes. It might be easier to avoid putting the 6th and 7th notes together. If in doubt, leave them out!
- Put imperfect cadence instead of modulation.

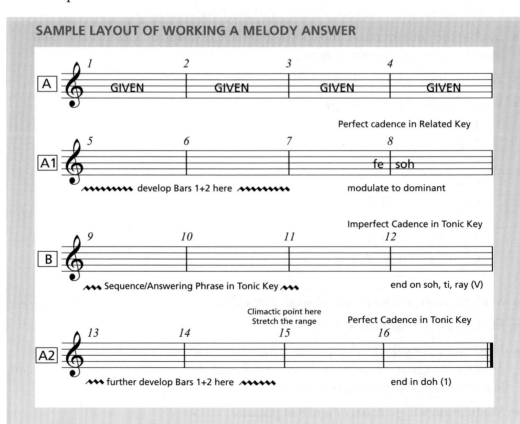

SAMPLE LAYOUT OF WORKING A MELODY ANSWER

1. Practise finding and developing motifs from the given phrase.

2. Work on phrase B: practise writing answering phrases/sequences.

3. Try stretching the range at the climax, e.g., 8ve leap or soh–fah (V7).

4. Use uncomplicated leaps, e.g., me–lah or ray–soh.

5. Avoid awkward leaps, e.g. fah–ti or the jump of a 7th (except V7).

6. Try to follow a leap by a step. Too many leaps/steps is awkward to combine.

7. Sing or play your melodies. Try to 'hear' your work.

Question 2: Setting music to a given text

- The rhythm and melody will come from the text setting.

- Read through the given text **many times** before you decide on your time signature and then on your rhythmic/syllabic structure. Each of the following rhythms could be used for a 6/8 composition:

HIGHER LEVEL QUESTION 1, 2009　　HL

SECTION A – MELODY COMPOSITION

Q.1 Continuation of a given opening

- Continue the opening below to make a 16-bar melody.

- Include a modulation to the dominant.

- Add appropriate performing directions (phrasing and dynamics) to the melody.

- Choose a suitable instrument for your melody from the following list:
  - ❑ flute　❑ violin　❑ clarinet　❑ trumpet

Sample answer

Watch out for the following:

1. Upbeat
2. Bar 4 is incomplete
3. Phrasing
4. Crotchet rest in bar 2 & 4
5. Pencil in upbeat at end of phrase A/A^1 + B.

(40 marks)

HIGHER LEVEL QUESTION 3, 2008

SECTION A – MELODY COMPOSITION

Q.3 Composing to a given dance rhythm or metre or form

The opening phrase of a gigue is given below.

- Continue the given opening to make a 16-bar melody.
- Use the form A A1B B1.
- Include a modulation to the dominant at a suitable point.
- Add appropriate performing directions (phrasing and dynamics) to the melody.
- Choose a suitable instrument for your melody from the following list:

      ☐ violin   ☐ treble recorder   ☐ flute   ☐ trumpet

Sample answer

9 Harmony Question

- To be familiar with syllabus requirements for the Harmony question.
- To learn the best methods for approaching the different options on the Harmony questions.

exam focus

The Harmony question carries **60 marks**.

The Leaving Certificate Music syllabus (1996) states the following Composing requirements for Higher level and Ordinary level:

2.2.1

At the end of the course, all students will be required to show sufficient understanding of the rudiments of music and aural imagination to be able to conceive and notate music using:

- both treble and bass staves
- the common diatonic intervals unison to octave
- the rhythmic values semibreve to quaver (including dotted minims and crotchets) and their equivalent rests
- the common time signatures (2/4, 3/4 and 4/4) in major and minor keys up to **two sharps and two flats (O.L.)**
- elementary chord progressions in root position as follows:

    chords I, V, IV, ii and vi – major
    chords i, V, iv and VI – minor

In addition, **Higher level students** should be able to recognise and to write music using:

- **compound duple time (6/8)**
- **major and minor keys** up to **four sharps** and **four flats**
- first inversion chords as follows:

    major keys: chords Ib, ib, Vb, IVb, iib

    minor keys: chords iib, Vb, ivb and iiob (diminished ii in minor key in 1st inversion – goes to V) and

    V7 and the cadential 6/4 chords (IC – V – I or minor version).

Question 4: Composing melody and bass from given chords

Most marks go towards the melody writing aspect in this question, so if you are good at writing melodies with passing notes, upper and lower auxiliary notes and suspensions/resolutions but aren't so great at working out chord progressions and identifying cadences, this may be the question for you.

Question 5: Composing bass and identifying chords from a given tune

This is the most commonly answered Harmony question in the Leaving Certificate and is also rarely in a minor key. Identification of cadence points, good quality and obvious chord progressions with correct notation of bass clef in the *given style* is needed in this question.

Question 6: Adding countermelody or descant with chordal support to given tune

If you are good at counterpoint composition and understanding and 'hearing' what your countermelody will sound like against the given melody, then this question may be the one for you. However, it is not answered by many students in the exam and it is perceived to be the hardest of the Harmony questions.

- The time allowed for the Composition Paper is **90 minutes**.
- Three Melody and three Harmony questions will appear on the paper. You must choose **one Melody** question and **one Harmony** question.
- Suggested time plan
  - Spend 5 minutes reading the paper.
  - Spend 25–30 minutes on the Melody question.
  - Spend 40–45 minutes on the Harmony question.
  - Leave at least 10 minutes at the end of the exam to check back over your work.

Harmony essentials

This section is worth **15%** (60 marks) of the entire Leaving Certificate Music exam (400 marks). **One Harmony question is worth more than all** the Set Works questions on the Listening Paper (only 55 marks)! Therefore, it must be given priority when it comes to balancing your study time.

As the key and tonality are given in the Harmony question in the partially filled in chord grid, it is therefore **vital that you understand how to:**

- identify cadence points and use correct cadence chords
- identify given chord progressions and use appropriate chord progressions
- harmonise in the correct manner
- notate in the bass clef (a common error) or write a countermelody
- use chord inversions where appropriate
- use V7 and 7ths correctly (7th falls)
- notate rhythm, putting bass notes in the correct position under each chord box in each bar (Question 5)
- fill out the chord box/grid or the scale with triads. Ordinary level students will be awarded marks for doing this; Higher level students will not.
- present your work in a neat way: neat musical notation is a must. Students should use a sharp B-type pencil when composing, as first impressions last!

THE HARMONY COMMANDMENTS

1. Identify which question you want to answer.
2. Study the given material in each question.
3. Look at the chord box to check the tonic key.
4. Plot your chords in the chord box and/or write out your triad scale for this key.
5. Don't forget you **must** use an 'm' sign for a minor chord if using chord symbols (chords ii and vi in a major key and chords i and iv in a minor key). Use small roman numerals when writing a minor chord and capital roman numerals when writing a major chord.
6. In a key with flats or sharps, you must use the flat or sharp symbol beside the chord name if needed (in flat keys mostly).
7. Be alert to given material with an anacrusis (upbeat). In the final bar, subtract the value of the upbeat from the time signature when composing.
8. Try to find the cadence points and bracket them. Find the harmonic outline of the given bars and structural phrasing of the piece (Question 5 and Question 6). This helps you to plot the chord progressions of any cadences.

> **RELAX!**
> Modulations will **not** occur in Harmony questions. In 1999 Question 5, the modulating box chords were filled in for the students. This has not happened since then and will not occur in the future.

Useful chord progressions

Below are some **good chord progressions** that you can use in **all** Harmony questions.

Chord ii usually goes to V:

- I – vi – IV – ii – V

  or

- I – IV – ii – V

Chord V rarely goes to chord ii

Chord I – ii – IV – V – vi

Chord IV – I – ii – V

Chord vi – ii – IV

Chord vi usually goes to either chord IV or chord ii

V can also go to I, vi or IV

Falling 3rds and rising 4ths are very good in the **bass line** but are also very good for chord progressions.

Never use the progression ii to **I** (common error at the final cadence) and Chord iii is not on the syllabus.

Minor Key Progressions

- Minor i – iv – V – VI (interrupted)
- Chord V – i – iv V7–VI (interrupted)
- Chord iv – i – iiob – V (imperfect)
- Chord V in a minor key is **major** and always needs an accidental **in front** of the note head.
- Can use chord ii but only in first inversion in a minor key (diminished) – goes to V.

Quick description of triad chords

A triad chord consists of **three different notes**. The **root** is the bottom (main) note of the chord and this is what we call the chord. When the root of the chord is at the bottom, all chord notes are stacked from this note upwards either on consecutive lines or in consecutive spaces. Example: C major triad.

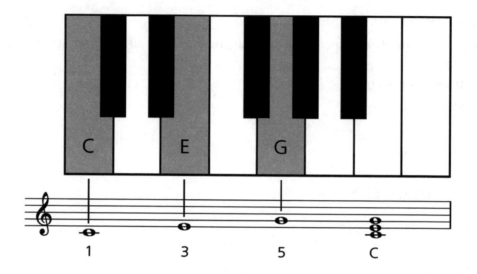

The major triad is formed by the **tonic** (root or 1st note), **3rd** and **5th** note of the major scale which starts on the **root**. For example: the C major triad is formed by the notes C, E and G.

There are four types of triad chords: **major, minor, diminished** and **augmented**. In Leaving Certificate Music, you only have to use **major** and **minor** triads, but chord ii diminished in first inversion (in a minor key) is also in the syllabus.

First and second inversions

If the 3rd (middle) of the chord is the lowest note, the chord is in first inversion. If the 5th (top note) of the chord is the lowest note, the chord is in second inversion. It does not matter how far away the higher notes are, or how many of each note there are, all that matters is **which note is lowest**.

key point

IN MAJOR KEYS, USE THESE FIRST INVERSIONS:

- Ib, IVb, Vb, V7b, iib
- 'b' means the first inversion
- 'c' means the second inversion

In minor keys, use:

- Ib, iib, ivb or Vb (chord V is always major)

Rules for first inversion use

- Use first inversion chords only in stepwise movement in bass to and from inversions, except if chord remains the same.
- Don't double the 3rd (middle note) of the triad in a major chord. For example: in a C major Question 5, if a note E is in melody at the start of a bar, don't use C/E as note E will also be in the bass under melody note E.
- Vb or V7b must always be followed by chord I (major) or i (minor) – unless the bass line is falling in step.

Rules for second inversion use

- Use only Chord Ic (major) and ic (minor) in second inversions.
- Use only in this following progression at a cadence point.
- Ic – V (V7) – I Perfect cadence.
- Ic – V (V7) – vi Interrupted cadence or in the minor key also.

Method of answering Question 4

Composing melody and bass from given chords

1. In Question 4, the melody and rhythm must be developed in the given style. This is a good question to attempt if you are good at melody writing.
2. After filling out the chord bank correctly with 'm', flats, sharps and V7, firstly, identify cadence points from the chords provided and bracket.
3. Start with filling out your bass notes in the given style. Keep the bass simple but don't use long note values in every bar.
4. Write your melody – it must be musically and stylistically sound and interesting.
5. Be careful of doubling any of the notes of the chord. Be especially careful not to double the third of the chord between the melody and bass notes (in major chords).
6. Try to use the root and third, root and fifth, third and fifth together. This produces better harmony (and better marks) than doubling the root every time you get a root position chord.

7. Do **not** use rhythmic ideas that are completely out of style with the given material. Be careful of your rhythms in every time signature, especially if there is an anacrusis (upbeat).

8. In a minor key, be aware of the augmented 2nd interval between the 6th and raised 7th notes (harmonic minor) of the scale. In an ascending scale, sharpen (#) each 6th and 7th note. Naturalise each note in a descending scale passage (melodic minor).

Method of answering Question 5

Composing bass notes and identifying chords from a given tune

1. After checking key and filling out chord bank correctly and carefully (don't forget chord V7, sharps and flats signs and 'm' sign for minor chords), firstly try to identify the **cadence points** (4 or 8 bars) from the given melody (insert a square bracket over the two empty boxes that you believe is a cadence) after singing the melody *in your head* a few times. Check for **sequences** in the melody part too.

2. Look out for a **modulation** within the melody (accidentals in the melody) and work accordingly. There may not be any modulation.

3. **Study the melody** (every note, not just the first note of the bar) under each chord box and decide which chords may suit. A chord may be in use for two or more bars!

4. **Write the chord** (choices of chords) above the empty box until you are happy with the overall chord progressions in that phrase. Be aware of **passing notes** (auxiliary notes) in each bar and **suspension/resolution notes at cadence points**.

5. Fill out the empty chord boxes in a **neat** and accurate manner.

6. From your chords, fill in the **bass notes** using a *development* of the given style. Be aware of patterns where **first inversion chords** may fit. Try to use some first inversion chords if you feel they would fit the progression.

7. Use **root position bass notes** at **cadence points**.

8. Double-check every bar when finished for accurate notation of rhythms in the given time signature, placement of bass notes and chords symbols.

9. Use only chord symbols **or** roman numerals – not both!

10. If there are longer sustained notes in melody, compose a bass (in the given style) with some **movement** (triadic or scalic with faster note values).

11. If the melody is complex, keep the bass line **simpler**. Add some occasional passing notes!

12. **Keep cadence points simple** with longer value notes.

13. Too many first inversions will make the piece sound weak, especially first inversions at cadences!

14. When finished, after 30–35 minutes, double check every bar, every note and every rhythm of every note.

15. This question is the best answered question in both Paper 1 and Paper 2.

COMMON ERRORS IN ANSWERING HARMONY QUESTIONS

- You do **not** need to add tempo markings, dynamic markings, expression markings, phrasing and/or articulation; so don't waste time doing this!

- You do **not** need to use chord iii and chord vii; they are not on the syllabus.

- In Question 4 and in Question 6, no marks will be awarded for **exact** repetition of given material or material that is much too similar in rhythm or melody notes written. **Develop** the melody and/or descant in the given style.

- Incorrect chords at cadence points lose valuable marks.

- Poor layout and messy notation will **not** help you to gain marks.

- **Inaccurate bass clef notation** is common, especially when there are two chords per bar. The bass notation must be accurately placed.

- Inaccurate bass clef (lower part) **rhythms** are common.

- Boring, long value bass clef notes (semibreves, minims) throughout Question 5 and Question 6 lose marks if they are not in the given style of the opening few bars. Having said that, **don't be too adventurous with your note values!**

Method of answering Question 6

Adding countermelody or descant with chordal support to given tune

1. In **Question 6**, first try to identify the cadence points from the given melody (insert a square bracket over the two empty boxes that you believe is a cadence).
2. Look out for a modulation within the melody (accidentals in the melody) and work accordingly. Sing given melody *in your head* a few times, even just to get the outline.
3. **Study the lower melody** (every note under the empty chord box, not just the first) under each chord box and decide on which chords may suit.
4. **Write the chord** (choices of chords) above the empty box until you are happy with the overall chord progressions in that phrase. Be aware of **passing notes** in each bar and **suspension/resolution notes at cadence points**. Also check for sequences in given bars.
5. Try to use some **first inversion chords** if you feel they would fit the progression.
6. Fill out the empty chord boxes in a **neat**, accurate manner.

When writing the descant or countermelody remember:

- Keep the range of this descant higher than the lower given melody.

- The melody and rhythm must be developed in the *given* style and must be musically and stylistically sound and interesting. Sketch outline of melody at chordal points.

- Be careful of doubling any of the notes of the chord but be especially careful **not to double the third** of the chord between the descant and given melody notes (in major chords).

- Try to use the root and third, root and fifth, third and fifth together. This produces better harmony (and better marks) than doubling the root every time you get a root position chord.

- Use **contrary motion** as a melodic device; also look out for passages where you may use some **canonic material** (imitation).

- When there is a more complex bar of rhythm in the given melody, you use longer note values in that bar and vice versa.

HIGHER LEVEL QUESTION 5, 2010

Q.5 Composing bass notes and chord indications from a given tune

Study the piece of music below.

- Insert suitable bass notes and chord indications in the style of the given opening.
- Do *not* repeat the same chord *in the same position* in adjacent boxes.
- You may use chord symbols or roman numerals, but not both.

HIGHER LEVEL QUESTION 5, 2003

Q.5 Composing bass notes and chord indications from a given tune

Study the following song and insert bass notes and chord indications in the style of the given opening.

- Do *not* repeat the same chord *in the same position* in adjacent boxes.
- You may use chord symbols or roman numerals, but not both. If you choose roman numerals, use *lower case* for *minor* chords

10 The Practical Exam

exam focus

The Practical exam carries **100 marks**.

1. First impressions are important.
2. Look and *feel confident* from the moment you walk into the room/hall.
3. Choose to perform pieces that are not too difficult for your ability. Choosing something that you can perform fluently and performing it well will build your confidence throughout your performance.
4. Controlled nerves are good.
5. Don't forget to breathe – not just singers, all performers!
6. Be so prepared that you can play/sing/conduct with comfort and ease, so practise, practise and practise.
7. No matter how you feel you have performed, this element of the exam is not over until you exit the room or hall. Last impressions are important too.

key point

The most important tip is to be *over-prepared*. You should be able to perform the piece in your sleep! If you are over-prepared, you will be as confident as you can possibly be, but you should not perform your pieces as if you are totally bored with them. All your pieces must have a musical **vibrancy** and life about them.

Performance requirements

If you are taking a Higher level Elective Practical (six or eight pieces), be aware of the *time limit* involved. Each student gets a maximum time to perform all of his/her pieces and this is also true of the aural/sightreading tests.

The standard required for your practical exam is gauged by five years of class-based learning.

Approximate timings
Ordinary level: 10 minutes.
Higher level (elective): 15 minutes (25 minutes in total).

What is expected of you
OL – Ordinary level. Two songs or pieces and one unprepared test.

H1 – Higher level, core (one performing activity). Three songs or pieces and one unprepared test.

H2 – Higher level, core (two performing activities). Two songs or pieces in each performing activity and one unprepared test.

HE1 – Higher level, elective (one performing activity). Six songs or pieces and one unprepared test.

HE2 – Higher level, elective (two performing activities). Four songs or pieces in each performing activity and one unprepared test.

Harmony, where appropriate, must be an integral part of group singing.

In any **group performance** (including traditional group), a maximum of **two candidates per individual part** is allowed.

Solo and group performing are regarded as **separate** performing activities.

Piano and electronic keyboard, acoustic guitar and six-string electric guitar, concert flute and traditional flute, flute and piccolo or any combination of recorders or any combination of percussion instruments **may not be presented as two different activities, unless one is a solo and the other a group activity.**

Accompaniment or duet performance is treated as **group performance.**

The same music may not be presented for two different activities.

Aural Tests

This accounts for **5%** of the overall exam (20 marks of your practical exam).

You can choose:
1. sightreading (on instrument or voice)
2. aural memory rhythm (clapping back)
3. aural memory melody (singing back)
4. improvisation.

You can choose to do these aural test on a different instrument (medium) from the one you have played/sung for your music practical examinations.

Get your teacher to practise the aural memory tests with you, if you are not taking sightreading or improvisation. These are worth 20 marks for all levels of exam candidate.

Past years' tests are available on the State Examinations Commission website: *www.examinations.ie*.

Sightreading

Look at the time signature, key signature and tempo indications first. Then quickly look over the music you are about to play. Ask yourself these questions:
- Are there any tempo changes, modulations, patterns, either rhythmic or melodic?
- What are the difficulties, if any?
- What are the dynamic indications?

Also remember:
- *Keep your place no matter what*, even if it means missing notes and/or rhythms.
- Go for an overall effect.
- Don't be tentative. Play convincingly; give the impression you know what you're doing.
- Stay calm!

HOW YOUR PRACTICAL EXAM IS MARKED

- Control of the medium: note accuracy and rhythm consistency
- Chosen music and standard of the performance:
  - musicality – phrasing, dynamics, phrasing and tone
  - interpretation – style, understanding ensemble
  - programme content – variety, standard and suitability.

11 Practice and Performance Tips

aims

- To learn the skills necessary for effective practice sessions.

Remember that your performance can account for up to **50%** of your Leaving Certificate exam, so you must give your performance the practice it deserves over the two years of preparing for the exam. **The best performers are usually those who use their practice time most effectively.**

Here are some tips for effective practice:

- Choose a time when you are well rested and your enthusiasm is high; for example, in the morning before going to school.
- A pleasant atmosphere, with no noise or interruptions, is most conducive to concentration.
- Try to find a comfortable, quiet place to practise.
- Good air circulation and good lighting are very important.

Self-evaluation is a must for improvement. Performing music is for the ear. You want to sound better. So, above all, remember to *listen to yourself*. Make your judgments and adjustments based on what you hear, so try to:

Record yourself

Record your playing often. It should be an ear-opening experience! You should record yourself at different stages along the way. Then listen carefully and decide what you need to do to make your performance better.

Advantages: It improves your ability to listen. You can hear and judge your own playing instead of relying on somebody else to do it. By listening to your old recordings, you can hear the improvement you've made.

Remember: Do it right from the very beginning. Always **aim for perfection** in notes, sound, and musical expression.

Try to understand the music

Look for the key, scales, chords, patterns, repeated sections, the form, phrases, accompaniment patterns, rhythmic patterns, etc. Analysing the meaning of something helps you remember it longer.

Write things down

It helps you to remember things better if you write them down. When you see what you've written a day, two days or a week later, it refreshes your memory and helps you retain the information permanently.

Create your own style by interpretation

Circle all the **dynamics** and **tempo markings**. Write in your music how you want to play the piece.

Look at practising as problem solving

Don't view practising as repeating your pieces a certain number of times. **Look at practising as finding and solving problems.**

Remember the 'five times easier' rule: It is five times easier to learn it right the first time than to re-learn it after learning it incorrectly!

Below are some recommendations given in the Chief Examiner's Report on the State Examination Commission's website (www.examinations.ie)

- Regular practice in preparation for the unprepared test is recommended in order to gain familiarity with the format of the examination.

- Students taking Music Technology as a performing activity need to be fully aware of the requirements for this option as specified in the Notes for the Information of Teachers and Students that is issued to all school authorities annually. In particular, candidates presenting Music Technology for Higher Level (one activity) or Higher Level Elective (one activity) should be aware of the performing requirement of this activity.

- Students need to take care when choosing a programme for performing.

- Particular care should be taken in the selection of keys for vocal programmes, so as to ensure that the songs chosen lie within the vocal range.

- Care should be taken to ensure that there is an appropriate balance between the performer(s) and accompaniment, where provided.

12 Electives: Practical, Listening or Composition

Note: Chapter 12 is for Higher level students only.

aims
- To learn about the different elective options in the exam.

exam focus
An Elective accounts for **100 marks**, or 25% of the total exam.

Higher level students must choose one elective from:

- **Practical** (done with core practical exam, around Easter)
- **Listening** (written paper on the day of the exam)
- **Composition** (portfolio work).

Ordinary level candidates do not have to take an elective. Their highest mark in core listening, composition or practical will be doubled to make up the extra 25%.

In general, not many candidates take the Listening or Composition electives.

Listening elective

- Read the questions carefully and answer what is being asked.
- Ensure you are familiar with the musical features of the chosen topic and be able to provide a personal response to it.
- Choose your topic carefully: it should be sufficiently focused to allow for detailed study.
- Aim for a detailed knowledge and understanding of your chosen topic.

Composition elective

- The standard of composing electives is generally very high.
- Your accompanying description should be sufficiently detailed. This is a syllabus requirement.

Glossary of Musical Terms

A niente – to nothing, e.g. to *ppp*.

A tempo – return to the previous tempo.

Absolute music – music that relies on its structure alone for understanding; also known as abstract music.

Accelerando, accel. – gradually becoming faster.

Accent – placed above a note to indicate stress or emphasis.

Accidental – a sharp, flat or natural not included in the given key.

Accompaniment – a vocal or instrument part that supports a solo part.

Ad libitum, ad lib – a term which permits the performer to extemporise or vary the music at will.

Adagio – slow; slower than andante, faster than largo.

Agitato – agitated; with excitement.

Al coda – to the coda.

Al fine – to the end.

Alberti bass – an accompaniment pattern of broken, or arpeggiated, chords; named after the eighteenth-century Venetian composer Domenico Alberti.

Aleatory, aleatoric music – chance music in which the performers are free to perform their own material and/or use their own manner of presentation.

Alla breve – cut time; metre in which there are two beats in each measure and a half note receives one beat.

Allargando, allarg. – slowing of tempo, usually with increasing volume; most frequently occurs toward the end of a piece.

Allegretto – a little slower than allegro.

Allegro – fast.

Alto – a female vocalist with a range between the soprano and tenor parts.

Alto clef – the C clef falling on the third line of the stave; mostly used by the viola.

Andante – at walking pace; tempo marking.

Andantino – a little faster than andante.

Animato – animated; lively.

Antiphonal – responsive music usually sung by two groups of singers.

Appoggiatura – a non-chordal tone, usually a semitone or tone above the notated tone, which is performed on the beat and then resolved.

Arpeggio – a term used to describe the pitches of a chord as they are sung or played one after the other, rather than simultaneously.

Atonality – lacking a tonal centre; music that is written and performed without regard to any specific key.

Augmentation – compositional technique in which a melodic line is repeated in longer note values; the opposite of diminution.

Augmented – the term for a major or perfect interval which has been enlarged by one half-step, e.g. c–g (an augmented fifth) or c–d (an augmented second). This term is also used for a triad with an augmented fifth, e.g. the augmented tonic triad in C major, C+, c–e–g.

Backbeat – accentuation of beats two and four, usually by a snare drum.

Bar line – the vertical line placed on the stave to divide the music into measures.

Bass – the lowest-pitched member of a family of instruments/lowest voice. Bass also denotes the lowest part in a musical composition.

Bass clef – the other name for the F clef.

Basso continuo, continuo, thorough-bass – the Baroque practice in which the bass part is played by a viola da gamba (cello) or bassoon while a keyboard instrument performs the bass line and the indicated chords.

Bends – a guitar technique in which a note is altered in pitch by pushing the string up.

Binary form – the term for describing a composition of two sections, AB, each of which may be repeated.

Bitonality – the occurrence of two different tonalities at the same time.

Brass family – wind instruments made out of metal with either a cup- or funnel-shaped mouthpiece, such as trumpet, cornet, bugle, flugelhorn, trombone, tuba, baritone horn, euphonium and French horn.

Broken chords – notes of a chord played in succession rather than simultaneously; an arpeggio.

C clef – a clef usually centred on the first line (soprano clef), third line (alto clef), fourth line (tenor clef) or third space (vocal tenor clef) of the stave. Wherever it is centred, that line or space becomes middle C.

Cadence – a chordal or melodic progression that occurs at the close of a phrase, section or composition, giving a feeling of a temporary or permanent ending. The four types of cadence are: perfect, plagal, imperfect and interrupted.

Cadenza – a solo passage, often virtuosic, usually near the end of a piece, either written by the composer or improvised by the performer.

Call and response – a technique of African folk origin by which a solo singer is answered by a chorus singing a repeated phrase.

Canon – the strictest form of imitation, in which two or more parts have the same melody but start at different points.

Canonic – a term used to describe a polyphonic style of music in which all the parts have the same melody but start at different times.

Cantabile – in singing style.

Cantata – Baroque sacred or secular choral composition containing solos, duets, and choruses, with orchestral or continuo accompaniment.

Chamber music – music for a small ensemble.

Chance music – aleatoric music.

Chorale – hymn-like song, characterised by blocked chords.

Chord – a combination of three or more tones sounded simultaneously.

Chromatic scale – a scale composed of twelve semitones.

Classical – usually music composed during the period 1770–1820.

Clef – a symbol placed at the beginning of the stave to indicate the pitch of the notes on the stave. The most commonly used clefs in choral music are the G or treble clef and the F or bass clef.

Coda – closing section of a composition; an added ending.

Coloratura – elaborate, ornamented vocal passage.

Common time – 4/4 metre.

Con – with.

Con brio – with spirit; vigorously.

Con moto – with motion.

Concert pitch – the international tuning pitch – currently A 440 hertz; the pitch for non-transposing (C) instruments.

Concertino – a short concerto; the group of soloists in a concerto grosso.

Concerto – a piece for a soloist and orchestra.

Concordant (consonance) – a satisfied chord or interval; perfect intervals and major and minor thirds and sixths.

Conductor – the person who directs a group of musicians.

Conjunct – pitches on successive degrees of the scale; opposite of disjunct.

Corda, corde – string.

Countermelody – a vocal part that contrasts with the principal melody.

Counterpoint – the technique of combining single melodic lines or parts of equal importance.

Crescendo – gradually become louder.

Cut time – 2/2 metre.

Da capo, D. C. – return to the beginning.

Dal segno, D. S. – repeat from the sign; frequently followed by *al fine*.

Decrescendo (decr.) – gradually become softer.

Diatonic – the notes indigenous to a key in a major or minor scale.

Diminished – the term for an interval that has been decreased from the major by a tone and from the perfect by one semitone.

Diminuendo, dim – gradually become softer; synonymous with decrescendo.

Diminution – the shortening of note values; the opposite of augmentation.

Disjunct – the term used to describe intervals larger than a second; the opposite of conjunct.

Dissonance (discordant) – sounds of unrest, e.g. intervals of seconds and sevenths; the opposite of consonance.

Distortion – a sound effect that overloads the speaker; used in rock and heavy metal.

Divisi, div – an indication of divided musical parts.

Dolce – sweetly.

Dolcissimo – very sweetly.

Dominant – the fifth degree of the major or minor scale. This is also the term for the triad built on the fifth degree, labelled V in harmonic analysis.

Drone – a continuous accompanying note usually played in the bass.

Duet – a piece for two performers.

Duplet – a group of two notes performed in the time of three of the same kind.

Dynamics – varying degrees of loud and soft.

E – Italian word meaning 'and'.

Echo – often called a 'delay'; a sound effect produced by a guitar pedal.

Embellishment – ornamentation.

Enharmonic – a term used to describe notes of the same pitch that have different names, e.g. c # and d , f # and g.

Espressivo – expressively.

Falsetto – a style of male singing in which, by partial use of the vocal chords, the voice is able to reach the pitch of a female.

Feedback – used mainly by rock musicians to produce a high-pitched sound.

Fermata – hold; pause.

Finale – the last movement of a symphony or sonata, or the last selection of an opera.

Fine – the end.

Fixed doh – the system of solmisation in which C is always doh.

Form – the design or structure of a musical composition.

Forte (f) – loud.

Fortissimo (ff) – very loud.

Fortississimo (fff) – very, very loud.

Forzando (fz), also forzato – synonymous with sforzando (*sf* or *sfz*).

Fugal – a contrapuntal compositional device like a canon.

Glissando (gliss.) – sliding, by playing a rapid scale.

Grave – slow, solemn.

Grosso, grosse – great, large.

Harmony – the sounding of two or more simultaneous musical notes in a chord.

Hemiola – switch between metres 3/4 and 6/8.

Homophonic – musical texture characterised by chordal support of a melodic line.

Hook – a memorable part of a song.

Imitation – compositional device involving much repetition by different voices/instruments playing similar material at different times.

Improvisation – music to be invented by the performer on the spot; used extensively in jazz.

Instrumentation – the art of composing, orchestrating, or arranging for an instrumental ensemble.

Interval – the distance between two pitches. The name of an interval depends both on how the notes are written and the actual distance between the notes as measured in semitones.

Intonation – a manner of producing notes with regard to accurate pitch and tuning.

Inversion – the turning upside-down of a chord or a melodic pattern.

Key signature – the sharps or flats placed at the beginning of the stave to denote the scale upon which the music is based.

Larghetto – slower than largo.

Largo, lento – slow.

Leading note – the seventh degree of the major scale.

Ledger lines – short lines placed above and below the stave for pitches beyond the range of the stave.

Legato – smooth, connected.

Leitmotif – a musical theme given to a particular idea or main character of an opera (also, in Berlioz, *idée fixe*)

Libretto – a book of text containing the words of an opera.

Lick – a melodic device based on a musical pattern to form short solos.

Major chord – a triad composed of a root, major third and perfect fifth.

Marcato – emphasised, heavily accented.

Mediant – the third degree of the major or minor scale. The triad built on this degree is labelled iii in the major scale, and III+ (augmented) in the harmonic minor scale.

Medieval – the period prior to the Renaissance, c. 500–1450; the period of the music of the early Christian church.

Melisma or melismatic – many notes written to one syllable.

Meno mosso – less motion.

Mezzo – half, medium.

Minimalist – style of simple harmonic music with much repetition of phrases.

Mixing stage (in a recording) – reproduces the sound and delays it.

Modal – scales that preceded the development of major and minor scales and tonality; gapped scale, whole tone scale, pentatonic scale.

Moderato – moderate speed.

Modulation – the process of changing from one key to another within a composition.

Molto – very; used with other terms, e.g. *molto allegro.*

Mosso – rapid. *Meno mosso*: less rapid. *Più mosso*: more rapid.

Motif – a motif is a short musical idea that occurs often in a piece of music. A short melodic idea may also be called a motiv, a motive, a cell or a figure.

Moto – motion. *Con moto*: with motion.

Multi-track recording – a technique by which up to 24 tracks can be recorded.

Natural – a musical symbol that cancels a previous sharp or flat.

Non troppo – not too much. Used with other terms, e.g. *non troppo allegro*: not too fast.

Nonet – a composition written for nine instruments.

Octave – the interval between the first and eighth notes of a scale.

Octet – a piece for eight instruments or voices.

Open fifth – a triad without a third.

Open strings – strings are not stopped, fingered, or fretted.

Opus, Op. – the term, meaning 'work', is used to indicate the chronological order of a composer's works, e.g. Op. 1, Op. 2.

Orchestral music – music written for a large group of instruments. These usually include strings, brass, percussion and woodwinds.

Orchestration – the art of writing, arranging or scoring for the orchestra.

Ornamentation – note or notes added to the original melodic line for embellishment such as trills, mordents, turns or grace notes.

Ostinato – a repeated melodic or rhythmic pattern.

Ottava alta (8va) – play an octave higher.

Ottava bassa (8vb) – play an octave lower.

Overdub – a recording technique in which another part is recorded over a previous part.

Overture – the introductory music for an opera, oratorio or ballet.

Panning – a recording technique in which the pan control allows the sound to be placed.

Passing notes – unaccented notes that move conjunctly between two chords to which they do not belong harmonically.

Pedal note – a long held note (usually tonic or dominant) over which various harmonies occur, producing harmonic tension.

Perfect – a term used to label fourth, fifth, and octave intervals. It corresponds to the major, as given to seconds, thirds, sixths and sevenths.

Perfect cadence – the chordal progression of dominant to tonic, in a major key V–I, in a minor key V–i.

Perfect pitch – the ability to hear and identify a note without any other musical support.

Pesante – heavily.

Petite – little.

Peu a peu – little by little.

Phrase – a relatively short portion of a melodic line which expresses a musical idea, comparable to a line or sentence in poetry.

Pianissimo (*pp*) – very soft.

Pianississimo (*ppp*) – very, very soft; the softest common dynamic marking.

Piano (*p*) – soft.

Pianoforte – 'soft-loud'. A keyboard instrument; the full name for the piano; it has 88 keys.

Picardy third – the term for the raising of the third, making a major triad, in the final chord of a composition which is in a minor key. The practice originated around 1500 and extended through the Baroque period (*tierce de picardie*).

Pick up – a small microphone in an electric guitar or other electric instrument.

Pitch – the highness or lowness of a note.

Più – more. Used with other terms, e.g. *più mosso*: more motion.

Pizzicato – plucked; on string instruments, plucking the string.

Plagal cadence – sometimes called the 'Amen' cadence. The chordal progression of subdominant to tonic, in a major key IV–I, in minor iv–i.

Poco – little; used with other terms, e.g. *poco accel.*; also *poco a poco*: little by little.

Poco più mosso – a little more motion.

Portamento – very smooth transition between two notes (nearly glissando-like).

Postlude – the final piece in a multi-movement work; organ piece played at the end of a church service.

Powerchords – use of open strings to produce a heavier sound on guitars.

Prelude – an introductory movement or piece.

Premiere – first performance.

Prestissimo – very, very fast; the fastest tempo.

Presto – very fast.

Primo – first.

Programme music – music based on a story, mood or idea.

Prologue – an introductory piece that presents the background for an opera.

Quartet – a piece for four instruments or voices; four performers.

Quasi – almost; used with other terms.

Quintet – a piece for five instruments or voices; five performers.

Rallentando, rall. – gradually slower; synonymous with ritardando.

Range – the notes, from lowest to highest, that an instrument may be capable of producing.

Refrain – a short section of repeated material which occurs at the end of each stanza.

Register – a specific area of the range of an instrument.

Relative major and minor scales – major and minor scales which have the same key signature.

Repeat – the repetition of a section or a composition as indicated by particular signs.

Rest – a symbol used to denote silence.

Reverberation – a recording technique that creates an echo effect using electronics.

Rhythm – the term that denotes the organisation of sound in time.

Riff – a repeated short phrase like an ostinato in a jazz composition.

Rimshot – drummer hits rim of snare or side drum.

Rinforzando – a reinforced accent.

Ritardando, rit. – gradually becoming slower.

Ritenuto – immediate reduction in tempo.

Ritmico – rhythmically.

Roll – on percussion instruments, a sticking technique consisting of a rapid succession of notes.

Romanticism – the period c.1820–1900.

Root position – the arrangement of a chord in which the root is in the lowest voice.

Round – like a canon, a song in which two or more parts have the same melody, starting at different points. The parts may be repeated as desired.

Rubato – the term used to denote flexibility of tempo to assist in achieving expressiveness.

Run – a rapid scale passage.

Rustico – pastoral, rustic, rural.

SATB – soprano, alto, tenor and bass.

Scale – a progression of notes in a stepwise motion in a specific order.

Score – the written depiction of all the parts of a musical ensemble with the parts stacked vertically and rhythmically aligned.

Secco – dry.

Semitone – a half step; the smallest interval on the keyboard.

Semplice – simple.

Sempre – always; used with other terms, e.g. *sempre staccato*.

Senza (sans) – without; used with other terms, e.g. *senza crescendo*.

Sequence – the repetition of a melodic pattern on a higher or lower pitch level.

Seventh chord – when a seventh (above the root) is added to a triad (root, third, fifth), the result is a seventh chord, e.g. the dominant triad in the key of C major, g–b–d, with the added seventh becomes g–b–d–f and is labelled V7. Much used in rock, soul.

Sforzando (sfz, sf) – sudden strong accent on a note or chord.

Sharp – a symbol (#) that raises the pitch of a note one-half step.

Simile – similar, an indication to continue in the same manner.

Six-four chord – the second inversion of a triad, made by placing the fifth of the chord in the lowest voice.

Slur – a curved line placed above or below two or more notes of different pitch to indicate that they are to be performed in legato style.

Solmisation – the term for the use of syllables for the degrees of the major scale: doh, re, mi, fah, soh, la, ti, doh. The minor scale (natural) is la, ti, doh, re, mi, fah, soh, la.

Solo – a part that is performed alone or as the predominant part.

Sonata – a solo instrumental piece (sometimes with piano accompaniment), often in four movements.

Sostenuto – sustained.

Spiccato – on string instruments, a bowing technique in which the bow is bounced on the string at moderate speed.

Staccato – detached sounds, indicated by a dot over or under a note; the opposite of legato.

Stretto – a contrapuntal compositional device in which imitative parts quickly overlap.

Strophic – a term used to describe a song in which all the stanzas of the text are sung to the same music; the opposite of through-composed.

Subdominant – the fourth degree of the major or minor scale. This is also the name of the triad built on the fourth degree of the scale, indicated by IV in a major key and by iv in a minor key.

Subito – suddenly.

Submediant – the sixth degree of a major or minor scale. This is also the name of the triad built on the sixth degree of the scale, indicated by VI in a major key and by vi in a minor key.

Sul – on the (e.g. *sul tasto*: on the fingerboard).

Supertonic – the second degree of the major or minor scale. This is also the name of the triad built on the second degree of the scale, indicated by II in a major scale and ii in a minor scale.

Sur – on, over.

Suspension – the use of a non-chord note to delay the resolution of a chord, frequently as it occurs in a cadence.

Syllabic – one note per syllable.

Symphony – a piece for large orchestra, usually in four movements, in which the first movement is often in sonata form; a large orchestra.

Syncopation – accent on an off beat.

Tanto – much, so much.

Tempo – the rate of speed in a musical work.

Tempo primo – return to the original tempo.

Tenor – instruments in the tenor range. It is between the alto and baritone parts.

Tenuto (ten.) – hold or sustain a note longer than the indicated value.

Ternary form – three-part form in which the middle section is different from the other sections; indicated by ABA.

Terraced dynamics – the Baroque style of using sudden changes in dynamic levels, as opposed to gradual increase and decrease in volume.

Tessitura – the general pitch range of a vocal part.

Texture – the term used to describe the way in which melodic lines are combined, either with or without accompaniment. Types include monophonic, homophonic and polyphonic (contrapuntal).

Theme – a longer section of melody that keeps reappearing in the music. Themes are generally at least one phrase long and often have several phrases. Many longer works of music, such as symphony movements, have more than one melodic theme.

Theme and variations – a statement of a musical subject followed by restatements in different guises.

Through-composed – a term used to describe a song in which the music for each stanza is different. The opposite of strophic.

Tie – a curved line over or below two or more notes of the same pitch. The first pitch is sung or played and held for the duration of the notes affected by the tie.

Timbre – tone colour or quality of an instrument's sound.

Time signature – synonymous with metre.

Tonality – the term used to describe the organisation of the melodic and harmonic elements to give a feeling of a key centre or a tonic pitch.

Tone – sound that has a definite pitch. Any given tone is characterised by length, loudness, timbre and a characteristic pattern of attack and fade.

Tone clusters – the simultaneous sounding of two or more adjacent tones.

Tonic – the first note of a key. This is also the name of the chord built on the first degree of the scale, indicated by I in a major key or i in a minor key.

Tranquillo – tranquilly, quietly, calm.

Transposition – the process of changing the key of a composition.

Treble – the highest instrument part; a boy soprano.

Treble clef – the G clef falling on the second line of the stave.

Triad – a chord of three tones arranged in thirds, e.g. the C major triad c–e–g, root–third–fifth.

Trill, tr – a musical ornament performed by the rapid alternation of a given note with a major or minor second above.

Triplet – a group of three notes performed in the time of two of the same kind.

Tritone – a chord comprising three whole tones resulting in an augmented fourth or diminished fifth.

Troppo – too much; used with other terms, e.g. *allegro non troppo*: not too fast.

Turnaround – a small harmonic phrase that links two sections or repeats of a piece.

Tutti – all; a direction for the entire ensemble to sing or play simultaneously.

Twelve-tone technique (serial music) – a system of composition that uses the twelve tones of the chromatic scale in an arbitrary arrangement called a tone row or series. The row may be used in its original form, its inversion, in retrograde, and in the inversion of the retrograde. The system was devised by Arnold Schoenberg in the early twentieth century.

Un peu – a little; used with other words, e.g. *un peu piano*.

Un poco – a little.

Una corda – soft pedal (left pedal on piano).

Unison – singing or playing the same notes by all singers or players, either at exactly the same pitch or in a different octave.

Upbeat (anacrusis) – one or more notes occurring before the first bar line.

V.S. or Volti subito – turn [the page] quickly.

Variation – the development of a theme by the use of melodic, rhythmic, and harmonic changes.

Vibrato – repeated fluctuation of pitch.

Virtuoso – a brilliant, skilful performer.

Vivace – lively, brisk, quick and bright.

Vivo – lively, bright.

Wah wah – a guitar pedal that varies the pitch of the note.

Wind instruments family – instruments in which sound is produced by the vibration of air, including brass and woodwind instruments.

Woodwind family – instruments, originally made of wood, in which sound is produced by the vibration of air, including recorders, flutes, clarinets, saxophones, oboes, cor anglais and bassoons.